MEMOIR

OF THE

REV. SAMUEL BARRETT, D.D.,

WITH A SELECTED SERIES OF

HIS DISCOURSES.

BY

LEWIS G. PRAY.

BOSTON:
WILLIAM V. SPENCER.
1867.

CAMBRIDGE:
PRESS OF JOHN WILSON AND SON.

The Following Brief Memoir

IS

MOST RESPECTFULLY AND SYMPATHIZINGLY DEDICATED TO THE WIDOW AND CHILDREN OF THE LATE DR. BARRETT,

AS A

TOKEN OF THE RESPECT AND AFFECTION OF ONE WHO WAS A PARISHIONER AND FRIEND THROUGH THE WHOLE COURSE OF HIS LONG MINISTRY,

AND

TO WHOM HE IS INDEBTED FOR HIS HIGHEST AND BEST ASPIRATIONS FOR MORAL AND SPIRITUAL IMPROVEMENT, AND SOME OF THE HAPPIEST RECOLLECTIONS OF LIFE.

INDEX.

MEMOIR.

MEMOIR.

THE character of a model clergyman — a minister, faithful and devoted, of the gospel of Jesus Christ — is one that must ever command admiration, and the most profound respect. A good man, a good preacher, a good pastor, he is at the same time a true lover of learning; a genial friend of education, — secular as well as religious, for the young as for the old; an advocate, by word and example, of private and public morals; and, above all, a liberal, wise, and firm supporter of public, philanthropic, and religious institutions. When such a life is closed, some memorial of it seems demanded alike by a proper respect for the departed, and the highest welfare of the living.

It is the object of the following Memoir to contribute something to such a purpose. In the absence of correspondence, autobiography, and other like material, the design of the writer is, that the ministerial and other public labors of the subject of it — his social, domestic, and religious feelings and principles as manifested in life — shall be made to reveal, of themselves for the most part, the leading elements of the character which is here attempted to be portrayed, — the character of a model clergyman, and a faithful and devoted minister of the religion of Jesus Christ.

Samuel Barrett was born at Royalston, in the county of Worcester, Mass., Aug. 16, 1795. He was descended, we are told, from an excellent yeoman stock. His ancestor, on the paternal side, was Humphrey Barrett, who came from England, and settled in Concord, Mass., about 1640; and, on the maternal, of David Fiske, who lived in Lexington, and was born 1675.

His grandfather was Oliver Barrett, who, after his marriage, settled in Chelmsford, and removed to Westford about the year 1770. Subsequently, he entered the army, and died at Albany, in the service of his country, leaving seven children. He married Anna Fiske, a daughter of Ebenezer Fiske, of Lexington, who was the ancestor of the many respected families of that name; among others, of Benjamin Fiske, the well-known merchant of Boston, recently deceased at Lexington.

The family of this Oliver and Anna Fiske Barrett consisted of seven children. Of these, Benjamin, the father of the subject of this Memoir, was the youngest but one. He was born in Chelmsford, 1770; married Betsy, the second daughter of Samuel Gerrish, an honored citizen of the town of Westminster during the Revolution. They were the parents of eleven children, only eight of whom lived to grow up; namely, seven sons and one daughter.

Of these, Samuel was the oldest.

Of his childhood and early years, we catch but here and there a glimpse. We learn however, incidentally, that he was extremely diffident. A portion of this diffidence was doubtless inherited; but the most of it, as he always believed, was occasioned by the treatment he received from his father's apprentices, engaged in a large tannery. Taking advantage of his extreme natural bashfulness, they made so much sport of his feelings, that at length he came to lose all confidence in himself; and it caused so much of self-distrust, that more than usual encouragement was necessary in whatever he was called to attempt. We incidentally catch another glimpse of him at this early period of his life. It appears that his sensibilities at this time were so acute and of so much depth, that it was found difficult to direct him by reproof without producing so much disproportioned suffering as to lead to extreme indulgence by way of atonement. Governed by the affections, he became firm, prompt, and active, as well as gentle, docile, obedient, patient. A single glance of the eye was command, a smile was reward. But he was not without acuteness and penetration enough to feel "that praise undeserved was satire in disguise."

In 1803, when he was eight years of age, his parents removed from Royalston to Wilton, N.H. As their removal to this place had an important bearing on the after-life of young Barrett, it may not be uninteresting to remark, in passing, that Wilton is a quiet, secluded, and almost isolated farming town. Surrounded by an amphitheatre of hills, the township lies, as it were, in a basin, the surface of which is dotted over with hills of a lesser grade; and these, gracefully rounded at their tops, slope away with a gentle, uniform declension, terminating in rich intervales. These hills and valleys, industriously cultivated, give many happy homes to a highly intelligent and moral population. It has long been favorably and widely known for its system of public schools, for its love of learning and religion, and as the birthplace of the Peabodys, the Abbots, the Burtons, the Livermores, and others, who have acquired no little distinction for their ministerial gifts and literary attainments.

On one of the hillsides described, stood the schoolhouse where Samuel, during the following seven years of his life, attending eight or ten weeks in each year, by unremitted diligence and application obtained more than one prize at the hands of the selectmen or school committee. Of these, the most valued of all, as he would sometimes playfully remark, as his chirography was none of the best, was "for having made the greatest improvement in writing." On the summit of another of these eminences stood the village church, of which the Rev. Thomas Beede, on whose ministrations he attended, and with whom, as we shall soon see, he was to be most intimately associated. On the summit of another stood the dwelling of this good pastor, overlooking the whole village, where, through his advancing days of youth, Samuel was to live, labor, study, and prepare himself for college; and where yet may be seen, still flourishing, more than one ornamental or fruit-bearing tree, planted or grafted by his own hand. And here it was, surrounded by the wild and picturesque scenery and the population such as we have described, that he received his first and most enduring impressions of knowledge, virtue, and piety.

It was at a very early period that he began to dream of obtaining a liberal education, and to talk of becoming a minister of the gospel. But, as the time approached for a decision in the case, the circumstances and probabilities became discouraging in a high degree. In 1810, his father, who hitherto had been prosperous, met with a reverse. He continued to approve of his son's purpose and aim, but could give him no encouragement or promise of substantial aid. Samuel saw, therefore, that, if he would still adhere to his early choice, he must not look to others, but depend wholly on his own resources and exertions. In other words, it must be another instance of the pursuit of knowledge under difficulties.

But it so happened, that, at this time (1811), his father formed the resolution, for the purposes of business, to remove his family from Wilton to Springfield, N.Y. By this unforeseen occurrence, the way was unexpectedly opened for Samuel to gratify the one strong wish of his heart. A consultation on the subject having been held with their pastor, Rev. Mr. Beede, it resulted in an agreement with this good minister to receive Samuel into his family, stand to him in the relation of a father, with the distinct understanding, that, by personal instruction, Samuel should be well fitted for college in the course of the succeeding three years; while the pupil, on his part, most gladly accepted the relation to him of a child, with all the duties and labors which such a relation implied. To this arrangement of sustenance, care, and instruction on the one side, and, on the other, of faithful study and labor conscientiously carried out by both, he often and gratefully recurred, as the means, under Providence, by which he obtained, not only the foundation well laid of a liberal education, but also a vigorous body and a healthy constitution.

He never failed to express the gratitude he cherished toward his foster-father and friend, Mr. Beede. On one occasion, he is found saying, "I have one friend: may God grant him happiness! What could induce Mr. B. to befriend me as he has? He could not have done more for a son: few fathers do so much." On another, he makes use of these words: "I cannot pass over in silence the continued expressions of kindness of Mr. B. I shall never be able to repay him for his goodness. May I ever feel grateful to the Supreme Being for such a friend, and some time be able to reward him for his disinterested benevolence and undeserved affection!"

It is hardly necessary to add, in this connection, that one so bent on obtaining a liberal education, and a responsible position in life, availed himself earnestly of every opportunity for improvement which the place and circumstances offered. At the suggestion of Mr. Beede, a "Literary and Moral Society" was formed in the town. It was, in fact, a lyceum, only under a different name, before the modern lyceum was known. Of this, Samuel was an original member; and by the questions here discussed, orally or in writing; by the use of the "Town" and "Ministerial Libraries," — both rare in those days, — and by other means there offered of mental and moral improvement, he acquired much valuable knowledge, and received impulses which enlarged his mind, and developed his whole nature, intellectual and religious.

In 1813, before the expiration of the prescribed term of years, he was prepared to enter any of the New-England colleges but Harvard. Before, however, settling definitely his future plans and course of action, he concluded, as his first and best step, prompted alike by duty and affection, to visit his parents at Springfield. Here, for the accomplishment of his ultimate purpose, he took charge of a small school; and subsequently of another in the village of Conajoharrie, N.Y., on the Mohawk River, which he taught for the term of six months. In the mean while, he carefully reviewed the Latin and Greek authors before read; and, as we have heard him humorously remark, "studied, with some considerable advantage, a leaf of human nature, — to him quite new, — in the life of Dutch farmers."

In 1814 he visited two of the colleges in the State of New York, — the Union at Schenectady, and the Hamilton at Clinton; but, not satisfied with either of them, he returned to Wilton. There, under the tuition of Mr. Beede, after four weeks of additional study, he felt himself prepared to enter Harvard College. Accordingly, in the month of August, he visited Cambridge for the first time, was present at the Commencement exercises, and after the usual examination, having failed in nothing required, was admitted to the Freshman Class of the institution in which, from early childhood, he had desired to be educated.

An ambition most praiseworthy had thus brought him to Cambridge. His studious and correct habits had secured him an honorable admission to the College, and he was cherishing a resolute purpose to prosecute his further studies with new persistency and vigor. But now it was, for the first time, that he found himself without the necessary means, or friends able to aid him on his course. Under these circumstances, but one way seemed open to him; namely, to adopt the vocation of a teacher. This course he at once cheerfully and successfully embraced, and pursued it, not only through all his vacations while an undergraduate, but for a long time after; so that, between the years 1813 and 1823, he had devoted to school-keeping enough months in the aggregate to make four full years in all.

When speaking on this subject, we have heard him remark, that, though the task was sometimes irksome, it yielded other than pecuniary benefits to the teacher, whatever chanced to be the proficiency of the pupils. To him, as to other teachers, it was a source of extreme satisfaction, in later years, that he could refer to not a few distinguished persons whom it had been his privilege and pleasure to instruct. Among others, we have heard him name such honored men as Judge E. R. Hoar, Rev. Dr. Stearns, Dr. E. Peabody, Warren Burton, Abiel A. Livermore, J. H. Abbot, Esq., Dr. Hosmer, Judge Luther S. Cushing, Professor Holmes, Hon. R. H. Dana, and others.

In 1817 he was elected a member of the Phi Beta Kappa, which, if any were needed, is sufficient evidence, we suppose, of his faithful and successful studies, and high standing in his Alma Mater. In 1818 he graduated, and received his first degree, A.B. For the occasion, the government had assigned him a forensic disputation with his classmate Walker; but, in consequence of the illness of the latter, it was omitted. The question was, "Whether uncommon sensibility to the pains and pleasures of life be favorable to individual happiness?" He prepared himself, with care, on the affirmative side of the question. "Give me," said he, "a fine sensibility to the objects of nature, to the emotions of friendship, to the sublimest, the tenderest feelings of pious devotion, and I can pity the world;" a genuine outburst of his natural, unaffected feelings.

From Cambridge, by previous arrangement, he went directly to Concord, Mass., and commenced teaching the Grammar School of this ancient and distinguished town. Here he remained for a year, during which time he was superintendent of the Sunday school connected with the Rev. Dr. Ripley's society. This was one of the earliest Sunday schools established in the Commonwealth; and it is not a little singular, that another of these schools had been opened in Wilton as early as 1816, while he was at college, which gave him an opportunity to witness the first dawnings of this beneficent institution, the knowledge of which left an abiding impression of its singular advantages to the youthful mind.

In 1818 he "began the year with the determination to live, in future, more devoted to God, more attentive to the duties of religion." Accordingly, at this time,—Jan. 1,—he joined the Church of Christ at Wilton, by receiving baptism, and assenting to the articles of faith. Not far from the same time, we find him prescribing to himself the three following rules: "1. I will pray to God, who is my Preserver and Creator, every day. 2. Not a day shall pass without witnessing my reading a portion of Sacred Scripture, if it be practicable. 3. It shall be my continual exertion to govern my passions, and form habits of moral conduct and pious devotion." And, through life, no rules of the kind perhaps were ever more conscientiously observed, alike in spirit and in fact.

In 1819 he returned to Cambridge, and entered the Divinity School. And here, again, it was a question of means, to secure which, he adopted the same method that he had previously found so advantageous. He began with a private school in Concord; then, in 1820–21, he took the Centre Grammar School at Malden, and, through the whole third year of his theological course, taught a select school at Cambridgeport, retaining his room at college, and keeping up with his class.

One who was a room-mate with him at this time, in writing to me, says: "We pursued together our professional studies, under the instruction of the elder Ware, equally revered and loved by us all; of Professor Norton, who had no superior as a critic and interpreter of Scripture; and of the lamented Frisbie, so earnest and eloquent, and whose early death left a void in the department of Natural Religion and Moral Philosophy which no one else seemed qualified to fill. To the faithful improvement made by our departed friend of these great opportunities, his classmates, his writings, and his ministry bear witness." With the termination of these studies terminated the obstacles with which he had had to contend; and, if knowledge obtained under difficulties is to be regarded as the most thorough and practical, it is well illustrated in the present instance. In 1822 he received his second academic degree, A.M.

Having closed his studies at the Divinity School, he was soon after, according to a custom of those days, "approbated" to preach by the ministers of the Boston Association. He officiated for the first time in the church of the Rev. Convers Francis, of Watertown. His professional labors were in immediate and constant demand, — first at Barnstable, then at Medford, and afterward at Eastport, in the State of Maine. In 1823 he was requested to go to Philadelphia, and supply the pulpit of the First Unitarian Church there, and also to preach to the Society at Baltimore, the pulpit of which had recently been vacated by Mr. Sparks. By arrangement, he continued for six months to officiate for these two societies. By both he was invited to become their pastor; but, in both cases, the invitation was declined. In 1824, he returned to Cambridge, and supplied various pulpits in that vicinity; among others, the new society in Keene, N.H., whose invitation to settle he also declined.

In all these efforts and decisions, Providence — unconsciously to himself — seemed to be guiding his steps, and preparing him for some important sphere of duty. At the period now reached, a movement had just been made by the Liberal Christians of Boston to organize and establish a new church and society for their nascent denomination. Channing, Norton, and Ware, with other distinguished clergymen and laymen, were zealously engaged in the undertaking. To this end, a site had been selected at the extreme westerly part of the city. In 1824 the corner-stone was laid in due form, and the building brought rapidly to completion. It took the corporate name of the Twelfth Congregational Society in Boston. In October of that year, it was solemnly dedicated to the worship of God, and opened to the public for divine service on the Sunday succeeding the dedication.

In anticipation of an organized congregation, the proprietors of the church, for reasons satisfactory to themselves, authorized the building committee to engage at once a preacher, and to settle a minister. Rev. Alexander Young, a recent graduate of the Divinity School, Cambridge, was the first candidate for the new pulpit. After preaching for a few weeks according to agreement, he received a unanimous call; but it was declined for another offered him at the same time. The State authorities had set apart a day, near at hand, for public thanksgiving (Dec. 2); and a preacher was needed for the occasion. It so happened, that the subject of this memoir, at that time a stranger to the people of Boston, had preached on the Sunday previous at Dr. Lowell's, in the immediate vicinity of the new church; his services leaving a most favorable impression. The committee of the Twelfth immediately sought him out, engaged him to supply their pulpit for that occasion, and also for the three succeeding

Sundays. Mr. Barrett, having accepted and fulfilled the engagement to the entire satisfaction of the committee and congregation, who had listened to him with intense interest, was invited, with entire unanimity, to take charge of the new society, and to receive ordination as its first minister.

After mature deliberation, he accepted the call, saying, in his letter to the committee, that, "prompted alike by choice and a sense of duty to yield to your wishes so unanimously expressed, it is now my solemn determination, under the blessing of Heaven, to consecrate whatever my faculties are, or may become, to the promotion of the spiritual improvement and comfort of those who shall gather themselves around the altar at which you have invited me to minister."

On the 9th of February, 1825, his ordination took place at the church in Chambers Street, as the first minister of the Twelfth Congregational Society in the city of Boston. The churches of the denomination were largely and honorably represented. Dr. Lowell preached the sermon; Drs. Walker and Ware, and Rev. Messrs. Palfrey, Green, and Parkman, assisting in the services. The exercises of the occasion fully sustained the reputation of those engaged in them for talent and Christian devotedness; and they left a most favorable and deep impression on the minds of the community. A new day, they said, was dawning in the world of Christian thought and improvement. Among the churches invited, the one at Wilton had not been forgotten; and no member of the council was more kindly and cordially received than was the Rev. Thomas Beede, the early friend and teacher of the minister elect, whose joyous and gratified feelings were manifest to all. To him was assigned the prayer of consecration; and it was alike appropriate and impressive.

The new minister entered upon the duties before him without delay. He foresaw they were to be arduous. The Unitarian controversy, so called, was at the point of its culmination. The church of which he was the chosen minister was the first erected in the city by Unitarians. The other churches occupied by the denomination had come into their possession by natural descent, and by changes in thought and opinion brought about by time and progress. There was good reason to think, therefore, that all the movements of the society, as well as his own, would be watched with jealous and scrutinizing eyes by opposing and surrounding sects. Moreover, a congregation was to be gathered, whose materials, wholly new, were to be harmonized, brought into affinity of feeling and belief, and a church to be built up and organized on a broad, liberal, and substantial foundation.

Upon this work he entered with energy and courage; and it took but a short time for observing and discriminating minds to discern, that, in this case at least, "the right man was in the right place." The people who had gathered around him, drawn together from different denominations in the city, soon found that the pastor of their election was not a stripling, just from the walls of a literary institution, with an unformed character and purposes, but a man — a true and a whole man — with a large share of common sense, with talents eminently practical, and with a degree of knowledge and insight equal to any occasion or emergency which might arise in the discharge of his many and responsible duties.

In personal appearance, he was above rather than under the average height, indicating a good share of vital energy and activity. Compelled, from a defect in the eye or eyes, to the use of spectacles, there was, at times, seen through them or under them, by the most casual observer, a peculiar expression, which spoke of insight or meaning, more than could many words. Blending with these were firmness and dignity, with courtesy and conciliation of demeanor and manners, which won from his people and associates an almost immediate and implicit confidence. A short time only was required to understand that he was one of those rare persons who think for themselves, and therefore are always ready with sound and sufficient reasons for the measures they propose. Offered with frankness and directness, they secured ready and cordial assent. With these traits and others like them, there shone out a perfect integrity of purpose, and a high sense of honor. He scorned nothing more than meanness; and the deliberate wrong-doer he repelled, if he did not wholly avoid. Later in his ministry, he preached a sermon from the text, "I am a man." It was much admired, and often repeated by request in other pulpits. It was a graphic delineation of the true man, without the slightest exhibition or consciousness of egotism. And yet, beyond a doubt, the moral elements within the preacher were, unconsciously, those from which the portrait was drawn. As he was at the first in this respect, so he was through life, even to the closing scene. His manliness never forsook him.

In the organization of the society, his first movement was in the formation of a visible church, according to ecclesiastical usage. In the presence of Dr. Lowell, who conducted the usual ceremonies and services, the pastor offered a covenant, which was signed, first by himself, and then by those present. To the reader of these pages, it may seem wholly needless and even impertinent to remark, that he who had drawn up and signed this form of faith was a Christian, — a Christian, not only by birth and education, but also from profound thought, and the deepest convictions of his soul. At the period, however, of which we are writing, under the violent throes of a long-continued and bitter controversy, it had become only too common for other denominations to deny the Christian name to those who belonged to this branch of the Church universal. But, as in all others, so especially in this particular instance, it was wholly unjust, and without the slightest foundation in truth.

This young clergyman, who had struggled so manfully for a liberal education, and to prepare himself for the Christian ministry, true to a sensitive conscience, and a mind logically inclined and trained, had not come to his work without reaching down to its foundation principles. His studies and exercises on the subject had been long and thorough; and he never ceased his investigations until every doubt had been removed. After a comprehensive study of all the evidences, internal as well as external, he was led to the solemn conclusion, that there could be no mistake as to the authenticity and divine authority of the Holy Scriptures, or the truth of Christianity as a divine revelation; not accepting these records, indeed, as verbally or plenarily inspired, but as containing undoubted revelations from God to men. Whatever, therefore, of moral and religious truth was distinctly taught in the Scriptures, and especially in the New Testament, authenticated still further, as he believed they were, by reason and intuition, he received, not only as true, but as the highest and most sacred of all truths, — God's. New theories, as they successively appeared, he carefully investigated and weighed; but, while they doubtless enlarged and quickened his spiritual aspirations and views, they never caused him to waver, we think, for a moment, in his original conclusions.

In despite of parental education and his earliest prepossessions, these united him with the Liberal Christians of the Channing school. Like them, he rejected the doctrine of the deity of Christ, and, consequently, the doctrine of the Trinity, because, like them, he could find no authority for it in the Bible; and if he accepted, as he did, the belief of the divine inspiration of Jesus, it was because he found it written there in letters of living light. One of the thoughts most familiar to his mind, and the one he was accustomed most frequently and energetically to express, was, that, if God had never broken the silence of the ages, — had never spoken to man, never revealed himself to the race, — then, of all creatures, we were the most miserable. In regard to all the other disputed doctrines of Christianity, he found himself, in like manner, coinciding with the earliest school of Unitarians. And with these intellectual conclusions were mingled feelings the most devout. In a diary kept by him at this period, the existence of which was not known, even to his own family, till after his departure, are to be found breathings and prayers of the truest piety.

In the covenant, therefore, which he had now offered and signed, were principles which had their basis alike in the teachings of the Bible, and the convictions of his own mind. The covenant was in these simple words: —

> "We, whose names are undersigned, do solemnly declare, that we believe the Scriptures of the Old and New Testaments contain the revelations of God to man; that we have faith in Jesus Christ as the Son of God, and Saviour of the world; that we desire thankfully to accept salvation through him in the way presented in the gospel; and we resolve, by the help of divine grace, to live in obedience to his holy commandments, looking unto the mercy of God unto eternal life."

He administered the rite of Communion for the first time in the month of April, 1825; and, from the beginning, it was made manifest that this was a service in which he felt, and was to feel, a deep interest. Though not gifted, as many are, with the natural power of extemporaneous speech, yet he always began it with a short address, — something rather new at that time, — which served to awaken deep feeling, and to leave impressions not easily forgotten. His prayers were short, but so earnest and sincere, that all hearts were borne up on the wings of devotion to the throne of grace; and his whole manner was so serious and affectionate, so natural and so pleasant, that every communicant seemed, as it were, carried back to the very scene and hour when the command was first given, "Do this in remembrance of me."

In his view, the whole efficacy and value of this rite consisted in the sincere love for the Saviour which it inspired and betokened. He failed not to preach on the subject from time to time, and on such occasions preached with more than his usual unction and effect. One of these sermons, — the first, we believe, — entitled "Excuses for the Neglect of the Communion," was published, by the American Unitarian Association, as a tract; and it had a wide and long-continued circulation. But further than this he did not feel it wise, or even right, to go. In his intercourse, therefore, with his parishioners, unless they introduced the subject, he was reticent; and they soon came to learn, that, if they were ever to engage in this rite, it must be, not to gratify their minister, nor to enlarge the boundaries of the visible church, but from a spontaneous love of the Master and his table, which was spread so freely for all. Nevertheless, the church rapidly increased, and soon became as numerous as others in the denomination. During his ministry, lasting thirty-three years, there were added to the church over three hundred members, — an average of which would compare favorably with most of the churches in the State or country.

His next movement in the organization of the society disclosed another leading trait of his character. By disposition and temperament, as well as from principle and duty, he was a Christian philanthropist. His heart was warm, tender, and benevolent. He had deep sympathies for the poor, the ignorant, and the oppressed, and a deep and persistent interest in all public institutions for the diffusion of knowledge and the relief of human suffering. The charities of his people, therefore, and their considerate and wise distribution, were among the earliest things that claimed and took a strong hold on his attention. For the attainment of these objects, he formed the male members of his society into a Benevolent Association. By the articles which he drew up for its government, it was made the duty of its members to ascertain the nature and wants of all the leading benevolent institutions in the city. This called out, for a succession of years, many valuable reports, embracing historical and statistical facts; and, by their pleas and recommendations, formed channels of a discriminating charity to not a few of the best of our philanthropic institutions.

Not long after, and again at his suggestion, a Female Benevolent Association was formed (1827), which went into immediate operation. If we are not mistaken, it was among the first of those sewing circles connected with churches, for charitable purposes, which, since that time, have become so general and so useful. It called out at once the latent benevolence of the parish; it concentrated their feelings upon the most deserving objects; and it developed the social element by frequent and profitable meetings. Through his whole ministry, he made of it a most efficient instrument of charity, in co-operation with its many earnest and active members.

In addition to these, he established in his parish an annual collection for the poor; and, as there were few or no recipients for it among his own people, he, with his deacons, became its almoners among deserving objects beyond the pale of the society.

But his benevolent sympathies were not confined to the limits of his own parish. He took an early and warm interest in the "Ministry to the Poor," of which Dr. Tuckerman was the first and active agent. Subsequently, he gave his earnest aid to the establishment of the "Fraternity of Churches," by which that ministry to the poor was placed on a permanent foundation. A constant attendant on its quarterly meetings, he watched and scanned all its proceedings with a vigilant eye, and was its honored President for six years (1852 to 1858). Indeed, he was never weary in promoting its interests. In addition to these philanthropical labors, it should be mentioned, that he was an active member or executive officer of quite a number of our public charitable institutions, and of these not a mere nominal member or officer, as is too often the case, but one ever ready alike to plan, to suggest, to counsel, and to act. And, in justice, let us add, that it was not alone in bodily and mental labor that he manifested benevolence and charity; but it may be said as truly of him, as it was of Charles Lamb by a recent biographer, that "he gave away *greatly*, when the extent of his means is taken into consideration."

In the further organization of his parish, one of his earliest movements manifested still another trait of his character; namely, a strong faith in popular education, especially of the moral and spiritual nature of the young. Very soon after his ordination, he began to lay broadly and deeply the foundations of a Sunday school. At this time (1825), there was but one school of the kind, connected with a liberal society in the city. But, fortunately, at Wilton and Concord, he had learned the nature and value of this institution, and had become its earnest, as he was ever after its constant, friend and advocate.

As a first step, he formed a Bible class of young ladies, to whom he gave a course of religious instruction, on a week-day, as a nursery for future teachers; and, soon after, made arrangements to meet the younger children of his parish at the vestry, on Sundays, at noon-time, for catechetical instruction. This was in 1825–6. Subsequently (early in 1827), he called a meeting for the organization of a more perfect Sunday school. Rules and regulations for its government, drawn up by himself, were cordially and unanimously adopted. The pastor, seizing the occasion, in words that seemed to burn, described the nature and character of the work in which the newly elected teachers were about to engage. The standard indicated was a lofty and spiritual one, expressed in language and tones betokening knowledge and conviction. Not a few were disposed at first to shrink from the duty as thus portrayed. But this standard, high as it was, kept no one away; and the power and influence of this address never ceased to be felt in the school. So true is it, that the human heart, in its best and calmest moments, is ever ready to respond to that in it which is the highest and best.

This school rapidly increased, became large in numbers, most efficient and useful in action, and maintained a high reputation to the end of his long ministry. Dr. Ellis, in his biographical notice of Dr. Barrett in the "Christian Register," soon after his decease, speaking of the Society, remarks, "that it had, for many years, one of the most flourishing Sunday schools in the city; and it was administered with fidelity in consistency with the modest but paramount objects of such an institution, by superintendents and a body of teachers who gladly co-operated in the aims of their pastor." And he takes the occasion to add, "that we need mention only the names of the late esteemed Mayor Seaver and of Mr. ——, both also deacons of the church, to remind many of our readers of the good repute of the Sunday School of the Twelfth Congregational Society." Occupying, as this school did, a large place in the thoughts and affections of the pastor, he was always to be seen promptly at his teachers' meetings, engaging in conversations and discussions, contributing able expositions of Scripture, and, in divers other ways, affording to the school every possible aid and encouragement. The children all loved him; listened to him with fixed attention when he spoke; and, by constant attendance and improvement, were emulous to win his notice and approbation. He enjoyed few things in life more than his intercourse with this school and its band of united and faithful teachers; and the recollections of his influence and labors in this humble sphere of usefulness must add much to the measure of his bliss in the higher sphere to which he has now been translated.

From a like spirit, his people at an early day were encouraged and aided in the formation of an adult parish library. Very likely, the idea of it was suggested by the "ministerial library" at Wilton, the advantages of which to the minister, to himself, and to the parish, had been so strongly impressed on his mind. It was in successful operation for many years; and diffused, among the young and old, a large amount of religious and general information. A juvenile library, a novelty in those days, was soon added, the books for which, for a number of years, were of his own careful and conscientious selection, and which, in after-time, ever increasing in volumes, became an unfailing fountain of delight and instruction to numerous and successive classes of children.

A like zeal he carried with him into other departments of education. The inhabitants of the ward in which he resided, spontaneously elected him for a successive number of years to represent them at the Board of the General School Committee of the city. Here, by his experience and practical knowledge, by his suggestions and assiduity, by his faithful examinations and other labors, he made himself a useful and important member. In a like spirit, his attachment to his Alma Mater — the University at Cambridge — was ever earnest and warm, his labors unintermitted, and not without their value. Of this institution he was an overseer, by election of the State, from 1835 to 1852; and, for fifteen years, chairman of one of its standing committees, — the Committee for the Examination of the Students in Natural Philosophy or Physics.

Watchful of her every interest, dear to him as the apple of his eye, he left nothing undone to ward off any danger to be foreseen, or to promote and secure her highest and most lasting welfare. In grateful return, she rewarded him with the highest honor, which, in his profession, she had to bestow, — the degree of D.D., in 1847.

Another prominent trait in the character of Dr. Barrett was his profound love of Christian truth, and earnest zeal for its wider, its universal diffusion. Entering upon the stage of life when the Unitarian controversy was in full progress and development, it did not fail to receive at his hands, while engaged in his theological course, under teachers who themselves were the leading spirits engaged in the holy warfare, a most thorough and exhaustive study; and, as we have before said, his decision was in favor of Liberal Christianity. While, therefore, on the one hand, the pure light of the gospel, "the truth as it is in Jesus," permeated his mind and heart with a joy unspeakable; so, on the other, the popular or prevailing errors in theology filled him with a sadness most profound, and against which his whole nature seemed to rebel. Ever uppermost in thought, therefore, was the obligation of every Christian to aid in the diffusion of the one, and to eradicate and limit, as far as possible, the life and influence of the other.

As an important instrumentality to such an

end, he was among the foremost to urge and advocate the organization of the American Unitarian Association. Established in 1825, he was chosen a member of its first Executive Committee, and was re-elected to the same office for fifteen years successively. In 1861 he was again returned to the Board, and continued in the faithful discharge of the duties of the office till the year preceding his death, at which time he declined to be a candidate. At an early stage in its history, he acted as its Secretary. In the discharge of the many duties devolving upon him in these relations, he was most untiring and efficient. His wise counsel, and shrewd and practical suggestions, were relied on as elements of success. The second tract published by this association, "One Hundred Scripture Arguments for the Unitarian Faith," was from his pen; and, during his connection with it, he contributed a number of other tracts of marked ability, all of which had a wide circulation. Some of them are still published.

In 1839, having obtained leave of absence from his society, he went to the West as a missionary of the Association. Absent three months, he made a journey four thousand miles South and West, travelled in fifteen of the United States, visited forty cities, and towns unnumbered, in that growing section of our common country; preached wherever there was a Unitarian pulpit; selected new fields of missionary labor, and gathered valuable materials for guidance in the future. His loving and liberal people supplied his pulpit for him in his absence; the Rev. George E. Ellis (now Dr. E., of Charlestown) performing that duty most acceptably. As early as 1827, he had originated the "Book and Pamphlet Society," assisted by the young men of his own parish, and of other Unitarian parishes, which, for many years, was an auxiliary to the Association for the gratuitous and widest diffusion of their excellent tracts, and other larger publications.

The same love of pure religious truth, and the obligation to defend and diffuse it, led him, as early as 1824, to become the editor of a weekly religious paper, called "The Christian," published in Philadelphia; also, to act as one of the editors of the "Christian Register," associated with Dr. Gannett and Lewis Tappan, Esq., in 1826,—and again with the same paper and other associates in 1840–42. He was also an associate editor with the late Rev. E. Q. Sewall, of the "Unitarian Advocate," published in Boston, 1830–31. His contributions to the "Christian Examiner," to the "Liberal Preacher," and other periodicals, may be traced to the same source. And it was to the same earnest and abiding zeal for the cause and prevalence of truth that we ascribe, in the earliest years of his ministry, the character and tone of so much of his preaching, in which, while special care was taken to spare individuals and avoid personalities, theological errors and false views of religion were boldly refuted and sternly rebuked, and the simple truths of Christianity urged home with great power and effect.

But, while he was thus laboring both within and beyond the boundaries of his chosen sphere of action, he never permitted himself to forget or neglect the most exalted and exacting of the duties of his profession, — preparation for the pulpit, and the services and solemnities of the sabbath. With strong and well-disciplined intellectual faculties, he was practical rather than speculative, logical rather than imaginative, wise rather than profound. With tendencies of thought like these, he was conservative rather than reformatory; but his conservatism was the legitimate and the true, which, clinging with tenacity to the good, the long and well tried, made him quite as eager to accept the new when it had been adequately and satisfactorily tested by argument or experiment. In all things he was alike liberal and progressive.

Dr. Barrett loved his study and his books. Few loved them better, or used them to a wiser or better purpose. A diligent and analytical reader, he aimed to keep abreast with the newest discoveries in science and theology; and, consequently, came to his preparatory labors with a full and ready mind. Always happy in the selection of his themes and texts, the latter were, at times, sufficiently quaint; and not infrequently he manifested a peculiar ingenuity in the development and management of the former. "Old shoes and clouted," and "Ephraim is a cake not turned," will be remembered as instances with singular pleasure by most of those who were his hearers, whether at home or abroad.

Outside of the sacred desk, as is well known, he was the most unobtrusive of men. He was ever ready to escape as far as possible from public observation. But no sooner had he crossed the threshold of his pulpit, than all his usual unaffected diffidence seemed to disappear. Once there, he failed not "to magnify his office." Forgetting himself and all that was outward, he immediately and entirely became absorbed and engrossed in the duties before him.

His presence and mien in the pulpit were peculiarly and eminently ministerial. As he rose to speak, Cowper's description of the true evangelical preacher would occur to every intelligent observer, —

> "Simple, grave, sincere:
>
> . . . .
>
> There stands the messenger of truth; there stands
> The legate of the skies! his theme divine,
> His office sacred, his credentials clear."

In utterance and manner, Dr. Barrett was unfeignedly earnest and fervent; distinct as he was forcible, — at times, perhaps, too forcible and too emphatic; but occasionally, especially in descriptions of nature, falling into an artless melody of tone, — which, combined, never failed to take a strong hold on the attention of his hearers, and left impressions not easily effaced.

Of course, as a preacher he was equally acceptable to all. Every preacher, every speaker, perhaps, has a manner or a mannerism, — a style of gesture and intonation peculiarly his own, — unpleasant it may be to strangers, but unnoticed or scarcely heeded by constant hearers. One of his recent eulogists has remarked on this point, "that he" (Dr. Barrett) "could not play very well on that vocal instrument, finer than clarion or violin; and, to those demanding nicely ordered gestures and delicately graduated tones, he was not specially attractive in the desk. But, upon some of us, there were few men who won so much as he by his delivery. It had the prime merits of heartiness, frankness, lucid language, and glowing thought." This is most truthfully and beautifully expressed. And of the most distinguished preachers of whom we read or hear, no higher or better praise is accorded. Of Dr. Arnold, of the Rugby School, whose praise is in all the churches, it is said by his biographer, "If sincerity and self-forgetting earnestness ever made an orator impressive, it was he;" but, it is added, "there were sudden gratings of his voice, which denoted, ever and anon, that his own warm and excited feelings were moved by the argument he was enforcing." And of Robertson, the great preacher of Brighton, England, we are told, "that, though he was carried away by his subject, he was sufficiently lord over his own excitement to prevent any loud or unseemly demonstration of it." — "It was excitement reined in by will, and made his audience to glow with his own fire."

In like manner it was with Dr. Barrett. "If sincerity and self-forgetting earnestness ever made an orator impressive," it was so in his case; and "if, ever and anon, there were certain gratings of his voice, it denoted that his own feelings were moved by the argument he was enforcing." Or if, again, like Robertson, "he spoke at times under tremendous excitement," "carried away by his subject," it was excitement reined in "for the most part" by will, and "made his audience to glow with his own fire." But, however this may be, certain it is, that it was mainly by the character and style of his preaching — fervent, evangelical, wise, and independent — that he kept his large church, notwithstanding the fluctuations of population to which it was peculiarly subjected, filled constantly with a full and appreciative congregation, through the largest, not to say the entire, portion of his very long ministry.

To make this delineation true to the life, or in any degree complete, it should be added, that, making no pretensions to the gift of extemporaneous speech, he would nevertheless go to his vestry, at appointed seasons, week after week, with nothing but his old and well-thumbed Bible in his hand, — as well known to his parishioners as his own person, — with a few notes on its narrow margin to assist his memory; and there he would pour himself out in expositions of some of the most difficult passages of Scripture, flooding his hearers with new light, and enforcing their moral and sublime truths with a power and eloquence, of a homely, practical kind, indeed, but which was sure to enchain by the hour the attention of his listeners, and who were made all the better for it the remainder of their days. At the communion-table, at the Sunday school, at the teachers' meeting, in speech, it was the same; not graceful, not rhetorical, according to the schools, but something far better, — having for its basis a sincerity, an earnestness, and a glowing warmth of unaffected piety, which gave to his words a charm and an influence far surpassing the proudest efforts of eloquence merely artificial and scholastic.

Other traits must not be forgotten. Alike by constitution and temperament, he was kind, cordial, genial, sympathetic, and warm-hearted. As we have intimated, abroad and among strangers, his diffidence from his youth up was not only excessive, but at times even oppressive. It led him to seek the retired corner, the back pew, or the lowly seat. But when at home, or among personal friends and professional brethren, his kindliness, his playfulness, his quiet humor, the warmth and frankness of his speech, made him alike endearing and endeared. Perhaps no husband, father, friend, or pastor was ever more respected and beloved than he.

In the discharge of his parochial duties, he was conscientious and untiring. In seasons of sickness, of bereavement, and of severe trial, he was prompt and ready. But these duties, always difficult and painful to perform, were met and answered on his part, more by the manifestations of his sympathetic nature, than by many words or outward professions; but the words spoken, few as they were, and all the more because they were few, made him a true "son of consolation," and gained for him the deep and abiding affections of his parishioners. An instance or two by way of illustration: —

One of his earliest parishioners, a lady, had set out in her garden, the year of his ordination, a rose-bush, and, from the circumstance just named, called it the Barrett rose. As a token of her regard, she made up a bouquet of its first and most beautiful flowers, and sent it to him. Ever after, as the season returned, she failed not to send him, from the same bush, though transplanted more than once, a like token of her continued attachment and friendship down to the last year of his life. Even then it had only been delayed for a day or two by her own severe illness, — delayed, but not forgotten. On the day of his burial, as he lay in the church on his funeral bier, the coffin-lid open, it was placed in his own unconscious hand, by a trusty messenger, in the presence of a numerous assembly who had gathered there to pay the last tribute to his worth, and to convey his honored remains to their final resting-place, — a lot at Mount Auburn, adjoining the lady's own, and which she had purchased long before, prepared, and presented to him and his family, so that her own remains might rest side by side with theirs.

Another instance occurs to us. A Boston merchant, residing in a neighboring town, became so deeply interested in his preaching, and so much attached to him personally, that he joined himself to his church, and walked to the city constantly (it was before the day of horse railroads) to attend on his services. Sympathizing with his pastor's earnestness in the support and diffusion of a pure Christian faith, he sent for him in his last sickness, and, as a proof of his confidence and love, devised in his will, under the advisement of Dr. Barrett, quite a generous sum in aid of feeble Unitarian societies, and made him its principal trustee. It is pleasant to remember, that among the last duties of his active and beneficent life was the preaching to some of these societies, and expending, through the labors of others, the income derived from this fund.

In the same direction of sympathy, kindliness, and courtesy, there is suggested another trait, which had a marked prominence in his character. It was in "his love for, and sympathy with, young men, particularly for such as were preparing for the ministry." From one of these we have this voluntary but expressive testimony: —

> "Different from many of his brethren, he always welcomed the new-comers! During the last six years of his life, I became quite intimately acquainted with him; and, although he was my senior by more than thirty years, in our walks together, and in our frequent intercourse, he was always so friendly, so loving, so joyous, that, were it not for his 'almond blossoms,' he would have seemed more 'brother' than 'father.'"

Another of these younger brethren says: —

> "There is no aged man whom I loved so much. He has been my good counsellor, my good friend, in so many ways. . . . He first encouraged me to enter the Divinity School. And what a benevolent friend he was to me while there! . . . It fills me with the deepest sorrow that I shall never again behold his kindly face, — never again draw near to his heart, so overflowing with Christian excellences."

Daily at the rooms of the American Unitarian Association, the common rendezvous of the profession alike for the young and the old, he was not only ever ready to extend to these young men, waiting there for aid, the hand of sympathy and welcome; but, possessing more than a common insight into character, he would discern, intuitively as it were, their latent capabilities or sterling goodness of heart, or both, and would seek out or make frequent opportunities for their employment and usefulness. We have now in our recollection more than one, who, long repelled and discouraged, were in this way brought at length into consideration and prominence, and became useful and valuable members of the profession, if not its burning and shining lights. Such loved him while he lived, and mourn him now that he is gone.

Another trait of a like emotional nature should not be omitted: —

"Nothing to me," said one who stood in near relationship to him, "was more beautiful in his character than his warm, tender love and profound reverence for his parents. Even after he had become himself a father, and his own head was 'silvered o'er with age,' he never forgot to make his yearly visit to them. How kind, how gentle, how respectful, he was! Father, mother, were sacred names to him. How he warmed and encouraged their hearts! The eldest son, himself a parent, he was a child there. No wonder, that at the last, both father and mother must have felt that there must be some saving virtue in the liberal faith, if it could thus exalt and beautify the character, and make so devoted, so dutiful, and so good a son as Samuel! * Respect and reverence for the aged of all classes was, I believe, in my brother, both an emotion and a principle. He could never brook in others any thing like slight or neglect of the old."

It was the same in regard to his fraternal feelings and relations. Though separated at so early a period, and at so great a distance, from the parental home and family, his tenderness toward them, and interest in their welfare, was never for a moment, or in any degree, abated. On the contrary, it was by his pecuniary aid, and other sacrifices, that three of his brothers were enabled to obtain a collegiate education; and an only sister, whom he tenderly loved, enjoyed the privilege, for three years, of receiving the instructions of one of the best of schools in the vicinity of Boston,— Miss Prescott's, at Groton. Strong proofs these of his true fraternal affection, of his high sense of duty, and his truly Christian benevolence!

---

* His mother died at Springfield, N.Y., in 1836, at the age of sixty-two; and his father, in 1844, at the same place, aged seventy-five. They were both members of the Presbyterian Church, of which he was a deacon. He is represented, by those who knew him best, as a person of more than common intelligence, integrity, and enterprise; and she, as of a gentle, womanly nature, modest and retiring, but one of the best of mothers.

But underlying and controlling all this natural diffidence, tenderness, and benevolence of feeling, there was an abounding share of firmness, fortitude, and high moral courage. In every case where the cause of truth was at stake, a duty in question, or a principle involved, he never failed to manifest the most unyielding resolution and quiet firmness. Nothing, in such cases, could move or daunt him; neither frowns on the one hand, nor flatteries on the other. As a case in point: He was a member of the ecclesiastical council for the trial of the late Rev. John Pierpont. He soon found that a majority of the council — among whom were some of the oldest and wisest of his brethren, those whom he respected the most and loved the best, and from whom at any time he would differ with extreme reluctance — were in favor of a condemnatory verdict on the many charges preferred against him by his justly irritated parish. Dr. Barrett did not hesitate to avow his opinion, that such a decision would be alike unjust and impolitic; voted in opposition at every stage of their proceedings, and used otherwise all the influence he could command to prevent a conviction. Defeated in this direction, he labored in every consistent way, so long as the council was in session, to mitigate the terms of the verdict. In this, he and his friends succeeded to their entire satisfaction. The final decision was just.

The same moral courage he carried with him to the pulpit. It is true, that in consequence of his general conservative principles, or, rather, from what he considered the dictates of wisdom and prudence, those topics usually called "exciting" were not frequently introduced into his discourses. As a general rule, he was decided in his belief, that such preaching was the cause of more evil than good. But when the fitting time came; when from some passing event of great moment, some stirring calamity or crime, the public mind was generally aroused, and partisan feeling hushed, and was willing to listen,— then, whether the subject was duelling or intemperance or slavery, or any other form of indulgence or corruption, fashionable or unfashionable, none spoke more heroically, or rebuked with a more intrepid voice: and his words were heeded all the more, because of his usual reticence and discretion. But not always; for we recall more than one instance in which pews were made vacant by his independent and decided reprobation of popular sins.

It was the same in regard to the late war. He deprecated a civil strife. He had hoped for a peaceful solution of the difficulty. But no sooner had the first gun been fired at Sumter, than he ranged himself immediately on the side of the North and of nationality, and never wavered in his convictions and hopes to the last. He hated slavery as he loved liberty, and, fortunately, lived long enough to see his expectations as to the war fully realized. His patriotism was one of the moving springs of his whole being. His discourses on the Landing of the Forefathers, on Fast and Thanksgiving days, were instinct with this spirit, and were models of their kind.

To resume our narration. In 1832 he was married to Mary Susan, daughter of W. P. Greenwood, Esq., of Boston, and sister of the Rev. F. W. P. Greenwood, D.D., Minister of King's Chapel, by whom, and at which place, they were united in the holy band of wedlock. This attachment and union was singularly fortunate; uniting him to a most estimable and accomplished companion, and securing the sanctuary of a happy home for the remainder of his days. They were the parents of eight children, — four sons and four daughters, — all of whom are still living, happy in the present, and prophesying, by their early lives, usefulness and true success in the future.

In 1839 there was a centennial celebration in the town of Wilton. It was an occasion of great interest, not only to its inhabitants, but to all who had ever dwelt in the place. The Abbots, the Peabodys, the Livermores, the Burtons, and the Greeles were there. Dr. Barrett was one of the invited guests. To him was assigned a part in the services at the church, and one of the speeches at the banquet-table. In this address he took occasion to pay a glowing but truthful tribute to the Oberlin of this "hilly and rocky" region, — him "who had poured upon his head the waters of baptism; from whose hand he had received for the first time the elements of the holy communion; and to whom, as pastor, instructor, and friend, he was under obligations that cannot be cancelled." And this tribute of gratitude was not limited to the individual, but was poured out with equal warmth and sincerity on the people of the town, "to not a few of whom he was indebted for acts of great kindness;" on their well-devised system of public schools; and generally on "the intellectual, moral, and religious habits and privileges of the town," — and closed with this significant query: "Moreover, sir, what town in the Union, of equal population, ever, in the same number of years, sent so few of her sons to prison, or so many to college?"

At a still later period in life, he made another visit to Wilton, and preached in the same ancient house and pulpit, from which, in his earlier years, the dews of divine grace had fallen so refreshingly on his own head. The occasion called out a larger attendance than usual; among them, the oldest inhabitants of the town. Indeed, the church was filled. As the services proceeded, and the people listened and hung upon his words, they could hardly realize, that this Boanerges, this prophet, speaking now with so much of authority and power, was the same person as the child Samuel, a pupil once of their former pastor, and whose call and spiritual culture had been received in this "court of the Lord."

At a later day, an intelligent lady of the place, one of the auditors on that occasion, said to me, "that she should never forget the sermon preached on the afternoon of that day." When asked the subject of it, she answered, "It was about the 'shield with the two sides;'" and then feelingly added, that "in her solitary moments, and frequently at other times, the thoughts contained in that sermon came floating back, and haunted her memory constantly. She only wished she could hear it again, or read it from the printed page."

In 1847, the society, in circumstances then the most prosperous, resolved to raise, by subscription, a sum amply sufficient to pay off a debt incurred at an early period in its history, and subsequently increased by repairs and other expenditures. The sum, though comparatively large, was easily raised, the society set entirely free of indebtedness, and the church "put in a state more gratifying as to its general appearance than it had ever before exhibited." The pastor gave fresh interest to his preaching by new trains of thought, and new courses of instruction; the

Sunday school continued to increase and prosper; and the varied rills of benevolence which he at the first had set in motion were not permitted to slacken in their course.

In 1850 he preached his "Quarter-century Sermons." In these, with a graphic pen, he recounted the origin of the society, its rapid growth, and its uniform prosperity and success. At the close of the second of these discourses, he set forth some of his own labors, with a modesty and reserve characteristic of the man, and took occasion to say, "There never, perhaps, existed a more united people than you have been. No root of bitterness has at any time, to my knowledge, sprung up amongst you. Like brothers and sisters, you have dwelt together in peace and love." This is the generous testimony that he bears to the conduct of his people. For himself, he adds: "I have been happy, possibly too happy. . . . Twenty-five more pleasant years than I have passed with you, have probably at no time fallen to the lot of another minister. Whatever awaits me in future, the past is secure; and I shall always look back upon the long portion of my life spent here with feelings of joy, tempered only by the sense of my own imperfections, and with fervent gratitude to Almighty God." And he closed with admonitions and encouragements of a most elevating, cheerful, and hopeful nature.

These discourses made a quickening and lasting impression on the minds and hearts of his hearers. By them they were reminded, and made to realize, as never before, the indefatigable industry and entire devotedness of their pastor, and felt at once how much he must need, and how well he deserved, a respite from his labors. Immediately and spontaneously they granted him a leave of four months; continuing his salary, and supplying his pulpit at their own cost. This offer, as he said, "generous as it was unexpected," he gratefully accepted. He availed himsel of it to visit Europe. He sailed from Boston in May, and returned in November. While abroad, he saw much, and enjoyed more. In the exercise of a natural sagacity, studying men, manners, and institutions, as well as objects in nature, taste, and art, he came home laden with the treasures and experiences which the Old World has to offer to the visitor from the New; but his heart never deflected for a moment from his allegiance and love to the latter. On the contrary, he valued and admired all the more the governments, institutions, manners, and prospects which the New had to offer the Old. He was welcomed back with gladness and joy. A series of discourses immediately followed on successive Sundays, calling together large audiences, who listened with gratified attention to the results of his wide observation and wise reflections under the new circumstances in which he had been placed.

His customary labors and duties were promptly resumed, and as steadily prosecuted for the next decade of years. And it is but just and proper to state here, that the appreciation of these, as well as of his talents and other gifts, had not been, and were not subsequently, confined to his own parish, or to his own circle of friends. As early as 1825–6, he had been elected chaplain to the Senate of Massachusetts; and during his ministry he preached, by invitation, an Anniversary Sermon for the Female Orphan Asylum, one for the Ancient and Honorable Artillery Company, one for the Asylum for Indigent Boys, a Dudleian Lecture before the Officers and Students of Harvard College, an Address before the Berry-street Ministerial Conference, and one before the Grand Lodge of Massachusetts.

This appreciation is further indicated by his publications, which were yielded to the press only at the urgent request of his own people, oftener denied than granted, or by others. They include discourses preached as above stated or in his own pulpit, discourses preached at ordinations and installations, sermons printed in the "Liberal Preacher," a number of valuable tracts published by the American Unitarian Association, and various articles in the "Christian

Examiner," the "Christian Advocate," and other periodicals.

It was under circumstances and encouragements like these that he recommenced after his return from abroad, and continued to prosecute, the work assigned to him by the great Head of the Church. But, in 1853–4, a cloud not bigger than a man's hand appeared to excite anxious solicitude on the part of both pastor and people. At this time it was that a current of emigration began to set from the portion of the city where his church was located, toward another section of the city, and to the surrounding villages, where residences either more desirable or economical could be procured. Judicious measures were seasonably taken to check, or in some way to counteract, this threatened danger. But neither the labors of the pastor, nor the zeal and energies of his people, could do much to avert it. The natural sources upon which the church relied for its usual supply were, by one of those revolutions not uncommon in great and growing cities, evidently and rapidly drying up.

In 1858, therefore, — the difficulty increasing so as to make some more decisive remedy necessary, — Dr. Barrett sent to his people a letter of resignation; saying, "Many things remind me, that the time has arrived, when, for myself, relief from the burdens of the clerical office will soon be needful, and when, without the aid of a younger hand and a fresher spirit than I now possess, the interests of our beloved parish cannot much longer be satisfactorily advanced."

This resignation was necessarily yet most reluctantly accepted, accompanied with such expressions and tokens on the part of his people as could not but have been most soothing and gratifying to his much-tried and anxious feelings. In view of his relinquishment of all duties and claims, on the settlement of a colleague, and as a token of esteem and affection, they voted him a gratuity of six thousand dollars, and bore "a cheerful and grateful testimony, that, with an evangelical earnestness and a vital faith, he had not failed to declare unto them the whole counsel of God, and to point out plainly and faithfully the only safe path to heaven, — a true Christian life; and, not satisfied with precept only, had endeavored by the daily beauty of his own exemplary conduct and character to aid them in the attainment of this great end: also, to his tender fidelity in the discharge of all his pastoral duties: and, finally, that by his constant and unabated zeal and deep interest, manifested at home as well as abroad, in the diffusion of uncorrupt Christianity, in the cause of general education and sound learning, and of every wise and philanthropic enterprise, he had not only awakened in the hearts of his own people a deep and practical sympathy in the physical and spiritual wants of a suffering humanity, but also, by the reflex influence of a prudence, wisdom, and Christian charity which had never failed, had done much to foster the stability and character of our best institutions, whether public or private, political, literary, or religious." Virtually, this was the termination of his regular ministry; but, in accordance with the terms of his resignation, he continued to supply the pulpit until a colleague was settled.

After a lapse of two years, — after the hearing of a large number of candidates, few of whom seemed equal to the emergencies of the occasion, or the wants of the society, — the Rev. J. F. Lovering was called, and received ordination at the Church, on Sunday evening, June 17, 1860, in the customary form. To Dr. Barrett was assigned the prayer of ordination.

By the terms stipulated in the letter of resignation, "in name Mr. Lovering was to be his colleague; while in reference to official duty, performance, and responsibleness, he was to be regarded as the sole minister of the society." From this time, therefore, Dr. Barrett ceased to be its preacher and pastor, only to become a proprietor and parishioner; never ceasing, as he had opportunity, "to mingle with them at their daily homes, in their private and public walks, and to favor them, as in past time, with his salutary counsels."

In a short time after, Dr. Barrett removed to

Roxbury. He took up his residence on the Highlands, in the immediate neighborhood of some of his ministerial friends, and of his old and well-tried parishioners. As his pulpit services were in constant demand, he continued to preach up to the time of his last sickness. He was at the Church of the Redeemer in Boston, so late as Jan. 21, when his subject was, "Jesus Christ, Heroic as well as Gentle." Rev. Mr. Bradlee writes, "It was a grand discourse, and gave great satisfaction." He visited the city from day to day, in the discharge of the many official and responsible duties which he had not relinquished. Daily he might be seen at the rooms of the American Unitarian Association, encouraging, by his presence and words, the new measures for the extension of a faith he loved so well, and for which he had done so much. Among other labors at this time, none were more interesting to him, or more characteristic, than his efforts to revive decayed, and to aid feeble, Unitarian societies, in which he met with gratifying success.

In the performance of these and other like duties, in the serene light of domestic affection and fireside joys, and the respectful veneration of all who knew him, at peace with himself and the world, with hopes full of immortality, glided quietly and usefully away the last days of this good man and Christian minister.

Through a long life, he had enjoyed an unsurpassed degree of uniform good health. As it was almost his first, his final sickness came upon him quite unexpectedly; but it did not find him unprepared. The spirit and principle of fortitude had been among the cherished studies of his life; and they did not fail or desert him when the season of trial came. His sufferings were continuous and severe for some weeks, but were borne with a cheerfulness of heart, a peace of mind, a spirit of patience and resignation, which flowed spontaneously from those elevated and divine principles which he had urged upon others in all his preaching, and by which he had endeavored to regulate his own life. His physician said "he had never witnessed, in similar circumstances, a balance more complete." Dr. Bartol says, "His malady was of a very painful nature; but he bore it with a hero's and martyr's mind, calm and clear."

Probably he was not fully apprised of the fatal character of his illness till the day preceding his departure. In the night previous, a vision of heaven, bright and beautiful, had seemingly been opened to him, which, in the morning, he described as far as he was able. He regarded it as nothing other than a dream. But did it not indicate a state of mind, pure, elevated, and serene, dwelling already in a region of blessedness, and catching a foregleam of the heavenly and the spiritual?

Early in the same day, a favorite hymn, at his request, was read to him: —

"Come, thou Almighty King."

When this wish had been gratified, he intimated by a few broken words — they were all he could utter — his desire to have read to him, from the same Bible which had been his constant companion in sickness as in health, the Sermon on the Mount. It was his last wish, but one full of the deepest meaning; for that chapter embodied the platform of faith on which he had stood firmly and confidently through life, and on which, as confidently and firmly, he stood in the hour of death. "The floods came, and the winds blew, and beat upon that house; but it fell not, for it was founded on a rock."

On the day following, — Sunday, June 24, 1866, — without a murmur or a sigh, this good man and much honored and beloved minister "fell asleep in Jesus."

In a sermon preached by him on the death of one of his aged and honored parishioners, he seems to have foreshadowed, in the following beautiful words, the time and manner of his own departure out of life: —

"Ah! brethren, the world is too much in our hearts, if we can never perceive the beautiful in death; and we do all, I suppose, sometimes speak of the beautiful in death, — the quiet, tranquil, passing-away of the spirit in Christian trust and hope. Yes, we do sometimes speak of calm, beautiful deaths, whether in infancy or middle life, because we, for a moment, see with the eye of faith. But no death is *so* beautiful as that which often occurs in the fulness of age. When it comes at the close of an upright, pure, and useful life, passed in contentment and cheerfulness, and not without enjoyment to the last; when the course of nature has been run; when the spirit, having trusted in Providence through long years, still trusts on, and sees no terrors in death any more than in sleep, and fears no more to lie down to the one than to the other; when the spirit so goes, life sinking like an expiring taper, or like weary, worn-out minds, — we see a fitness, nay, a sort of natural beauty, in the event."

> "So fades a summer cloud away,
> So sinks the gale when storms are o'er,
> So gently shuts the eye of day,
> So dies a wave along the shore.
>
> Life's duty done, as sinks the clay,
> Light from the load the spirit flies;
> While heaven and earth combine to say,
> 'How blest the righteous when he dies!'"

The funeral was attended on the following Tuesday, at the church of Dr. Putnam, Roxbury. A large assemblage were present to testify their respect for the memory of the departed. As he lay in his coffin, the features of the deceased were placid and sweet almost beyond expression. They were saint-like. The peace of heaven seemed to have settled down on them. Drs. Lothrop, Bartol, and Gannett conducted the services of the occasion, — hymns, address, and prayer, — evincing a just and tender appreciation of the labors, life, and character of their departed brother, and the loss sustained by the community. The music of the choir and organ harmonized and deepened the feelings of the whole audience, and the scene was one long to be remembered. He was borne to his last resting-place at Mount Auburn, followed by a long train of sympathizing friends, among whom none were deeper or more sincere mourners than the former members of the Twelfth Congregational Society, of which he was sole minister for thirty-five years; one of the longest pastorates on record in the city of Boston, out of more than two hundred ministers settled there during the present century.

Since that time, the members of his former flock have subscribed, almost spontaneously, a sum of money fully adequate for the purchase of an appropriate and handsome monument to be erected over his grave the coming season, with appropriate ornamentation and inscriptions, as a testimonial of their unabated gratitude for his consecrated labors of many years, and of continued affection and respect for his character and memory.

APPENDIX TO MEMOIR.

I.

It was natural, as it was just, that one who, through his whole life, had been so tender of the feelings and reputations of others, — never failing to rebuke the censorious, whether of the living or the dead, — and whose joy and custom it was to commend at all proper times, and with all fitting words, the deserving and the good, should, at his decease, have many to rise up spontaneously, to do him honor with their pens, and to drop the tear and the myrtle wreath upon his grave.

On the announcement, therefore, of his decease, obituary notices appeared in most of the papers and periodicals, not only in the city, but elsewhere; some of them elaborate, all of them highly and justly appreciative. To give more of fulness and completeness to this otherwise imperfect Memoir, we subjoin here brief abstracts of some of these sketches, and, with these, extracts from a few letters in our possession, through which we shall obtain additional estimates, and some new and interesting traits, of Dr. Barrett's character.

From the notice in the "Christian Register," attributed to the Rev. G. E. Ellis, D.D., so discriminating and so just, we give this short abstract: —

"He was one of the narrowing circle of the wise and good, the constant and experienced, the friendly and judicious, of our elder brethren, on whom we feel we are depending with an affectionate confidence, amid changes which take away more than they supply of enthusiasm and courage of heart. So admirably poised in him was the balance between a love of the old, and a hospitality towards the new, elements of the working religious forces of the age, that there is hardly another of the elders among us who may more fairly represent the creed and spirit of our fellowship. . . . We know not, indeed, that in his personal convictions, or in the sum or substance of his Christian opinions, he had yielded to any essential modification of the views with which he entered upon his ministry. But he doubtless had learned to adjust his early creed to the expanding influences of modern criticism and speculation. . . . As pastor, he was most assiduous and single-hearted; he wrought faithfully in routine and systematic methods, and was ready to vary, according to new conditions, the stereotyped course of the ministry. He kept abreast of the times, and, though he loved quiet, did not shun the peaceful agitation of novelties. His own sterling qualities of character — right-heartedness, sound judgment, and gentle kindness of spirit — secured him willing helpers. . . . His advice was sought by those who intended to follow it if they could get it. He had no petty jealousies, no pestering suspicions, no side self-seekings. . . . He united the dignities of a philosophic calm with the graces of a Christian humility and serenity. . . .

"As a preacher, Dr. Barrett was regarded by his own people as having but few, if any, superiors in the effectiveness of his pulpit ministrations. . . . He felt deeply the truth and the importance of the views he presented; and he chose his themes with a reference to the seriousness and the practical power which they ought to have for intelligent and well-disposed persons. . . . He spoke from a full mind, as he continued to be a diligent reader. Good sense, moderation, substantial matter, and the simple desire for edification, characterized his compositions. He was also a sagacious observer of men; and his eyes and mind were always open to the teachings of the living world.

"Among his brethren, Dr. Barrett held a high place of respect and confidence. His modesty and unobtrusiveness of spirit made him rather a listener than a frequent speaker in their meetings. . . . He was a kindly critic.

"Nor did Dr. Barrett confine his interest in the cause of Christian truth to his well-served work in his own parish. He was one of the early members of the American Unitarian Association. To his wisdom and discreet judgment that Association was indebted from its very beginning, and it retained his interest in the new promise of its activity and accomplishments. When he entered upon his ministry, the need of controversy, and the championship of contested Christian liberty, required of him and his brethren a kind of zeal which is not so much needed — not to say so well appreciated — in these days. . . . He dealt some hard blows, but followed them with his mild and kind wishes, with the hope that they would injure only the errors, and not those who hold them; for he was not a man of stern or severe spirit.

"Now, we trust, he is among the forgiven and the glorified. Pleasantly and lovingly shall we cherish the image and memory which he has left us."

From a sermon preached by Dr. Bartol from his own pulpit, West Church, Boston, a few Sundays after the interment, and subsequently published in the "Monthly Religious Magazine," we select the following sentences, embracing a brief summary of his views of Dr. Barrett's life and character : —

"Dr. Barrett was a good man. There was nothing about him cold, indifferent, or tame, rather an extraordinary fervor. But his heart had no foul or malign element. His fire showed the purity of a smokeless flame. It was fed with no selfish or sensual fire, but sacred essences of humanity and truth. Let me bear him witness! Throughout these thirty years of our mutual acquaintance, I never met him but to see this divine ardor in his face, hear it in his voice, and mark it in his manner; and to breathe in his whole atmosphere that indescribable blending of beautiful traits, the secret of whose unity could no more be detected than the way the seven colors melt into the spotless white. So gentle his look, so cordial his greeting, it was sufficient to imagine that an almost volcanic passion was native to his soul. But never was victory more perfect than in the charity to which his temper was schooled and subdued.

"The combination, too, in character, so rare and hard, of the *kind* with the *sincere*, in him was complete. . . . His veracity seemed a law. He did not know how to tell a lie. I do not think he could have done it. Yet there was no attribute in him his friends would perhaps sooner single out than his wisdom, though it was wisdom without suspicion of management or cunning. . . . He was simple as he was wise. With shrewdness, I should say, he united self-forgetfulness, but that there appeared no *self* to forget. Self-denial was self-indulgence. His entire self-government set him against all violent procedure, even in reform. Yet, though late in the field, he was loyal to the core; for when the enemies of freedom showed their hand, and began to play with guns their terrible game, none resisted with more resolution.

"Bright and cheering views his own mind moved him to take. To him, in his goodness, all was good. The world was a good world; the race was a good race; all fortune was good fortune; and Providence was infinitely good. In the darkest times, he never despaired. . . . I suppose there never was profounder faith in the future of mankind, and the immortal destiny and bliss of the children of men. . . .

"Never was pity more tender or reflective or circumspect. I should leave out one of his principal traits, if I omitted this uniform, unsurpassed forbearance to rub unnecessarily the sore spot. . . . Not that he was reticent or close. He was transparent and altogether decided in his opinion. But he differed entirely from those who are diligent to thrust in the probe where they have not been called as surgeons, and chafing into morbid activity old and half-healed wounds. The young are good judges; and he singularly drew them, as a teacher, in early life. . . .

"He was a good man. Perhaps no clergyman has been more beloved by his parishioners and professional associates. Many a heart was in the coffin holding the precious remains that had been his body, — the shrine of a nature as noble and affectionate as is ever dressed in human form, still keeping in decay his innocent and generous look."

One of his classmates, while at the Divinity School, has favored us with this brief estimate of Dr. Barrett's character: —

"He was a diligent student, and ranked high as a scholar. His research was thorough, his judgment discriminating and independent, and his conclusions held and defended without narrowness or bigotry. Possessing more than ordinary abilities, had he been ambitious of distinction and less diffident of himself, he would doubtless have taken rank among the foremost in his profession. His probity, sincerity, goodness of heart, and constancy in friendship, won for him the respect, confidence, and love of all who knew him. To me, his memory is endeared by many a fond remembrance."

From the Records of the Society for the Relief of Destitute Clergymen: —

"BOSTON, NOV. 5, 1866.

"Attention having been called to the vacancy in the Executive Committee occasioned by the death of the Rev. Dr. Barrett, the following resolution was proposed by President Walker, and passed unanimously: —

"*Resolved,* That we cannot refrain from recording our sense of the loss this Society has sustained in the death of one of its earliest and best friends, our profound respect for our late associate, and our personal regret that we are no longer to have the benefit of his council and co-operation in the work before us."

Rev. Dr. Miles, Secretary of the Society for promoting Theological Education at Cambridge, writes of Dr. Barrett thus: "I need not say to you, who knew his faithfulness so well, that there was hardly any member more constant in his attendance on its meetings, or more watchful of its interests;" and then takes occasion to add: "Equally needless must it be for me to assure you of the respectful deference with which his opinions were always received and often asked; uttered, as they were, positively but modestly, kindly, and often playfully, and with an unfailing good sense and judgment. There was the interest of decision in all that he said. No one was left in doubt where he stood. The conclusions, so squarely defined, were seen to be the fruit of sagacious thought, and always had a broad and generous basis. If others had more book-learning, there have been few among the clergy who had a more practical knowledge of mankind. I do not think he has left one who surpassed him in the warmth of personal affection with which he was universally regarded." This he writes after an "affectionate intimacy of nearly forty years."

Rev. Charles Brooks writes me, "I once made a study of his character; and I could not find any more fault with it than I could with the law of gravitation."

The following testimonial is from another of his professional brethren, one who knew him long and well, writing to another venerable brother, who perhaps knew him still better: —

"You and I have parted for a while — a little while — with a very dear and pleasant friend; one whose cordiality, kindness, and faithfulness rendered his friendship of inestimable worth to us; one with whose name and memory will be mingled sacred and delightful associations. Very pleasant was his social intercourse; very grateful his cordial and kindly greetings; impressive his many wise, and exhilarating his mirthful and witty, sayings. We shall never forget what he was to us in our frequent meetings. But especially shall we cherish and venerate his memory and name as that of a good man, — a faithful, devoted, beloved, and most successful minister of the Lord Jesus Christ, — eminently deserving the tender and affectionate remembrance which drew forth so many tears at his funeral. Let us often think, —

'We die not all; for myriad beings,
That live and think and do,
Have felt our life, in its secret springs,
And will feel it their being through.

We die not all: we shall live on earth,
In the words and deeds of the past;
And death to the soul is a glorious birth,
Where no seeds of decay are cast.'"

II.

A COMPLETE LIST OF DR. BARRETT'S PUBLISHED WRITINGS.

1825. Review of Rev. E. Q. Sewall's Sermon on Human Depravity. Ch. Ex., vol. ii. pp. 285–90.

1825. One Hundred Scriptural Arguments for the Unitarian Faith. Tract No. 2, A. U. A.

1826. Review of Noyes's Amended Version of the Book of Job. Ch. Ex., vol. iv.

1828. The Apostle Peter a Unitarian. Tract No. 55, A. U. A.

1829. Excuses for the Neglect of the Communion considered. Tract No. 22, A. U. A.

1829. Sermon, Ordination of Rev. M. G. Thomas, Concord, N .H. Boston: L. C. Bowles.

1829. A Tract, No. 28, A. U. A.; title, "The Doctrine of Religious Experience."

1831. Sermon, "Our Obligations and Privileges as Christians." Vol. i. No. 4, Liberal Preacher.

1831. Discourse before the Ancient and Honorable Artillery Company. Published at Cambridge: Metcalf & Co.

1832. Sermon at Twelfth Congregational Society, Fast Day: Cholera. Hillard, Gray, & Co.

1833. Sermon, "The Kingdom of God Within." Lib. P., vol. iii. No. 5, New Series.

1834. Sermon, Installation of Rev. G. R. Noyes at Petersham. Chas. Bowen.

1834. Tract No. 90, "Apologies for Indifference to Religion, &c., examined." A. U. A.

1835. Address, Grand Lodge of Massachusetts: "Character of St. John the Evangelist."

1838. Sermon, Twelfth Congregational Society, on Duelling. Boston: I. R. Butts. pp. 18.

1839. Speech at the Centennial Celebration, Wilton. Boston: B. H. Greene.

1843. Sermon, "What Thinkest Thou? or, Ten Questions Answered." Tract No. 190, A. U. A.

1845. Review of "Life and Discourses of Rev. G. W. Wells." Ch. Ex., 4th series, March No.

1845. Reflections in a Sunday School. Tuttle & Dennett.

1847. "Relation of Liberal Christians to our Age and Country." Address before Min. Con. Ch. Ex., vol. viii. 4th series, Sept. No.

1847. Review of the Life, Character, and Select Works of Elder Simon Clough. Ch. Ex., vol. vii.

1848. A Tract, No. 246, A. U. A.: "What becomes me, &c.?"

1850. Two Discourses on the Completion of the Twenty-fifth Year of his Ministry. pp. 40. Boston: Tuttle & Dennett.

1857. "Youths Void of Understanding." Discourse, Twelfth Congregational Society, March, 1857. Boston: Crosby & Nichols.

OFFICES HELD BY DR. BARRETT.

18— to 18—. Secretary of the Berry-street Conference of Ministers.

1825 to 1841. Executive Committee of the American Unitarian Association.

1862 to 1866. Same.

1834 to 1858. Member of the Executive Committee Massachusetts Evangelical Missionary Society.

1858 to 1866. Vice-President of the same.

1842 to 1866. Member of the Select Committee of the Society for Propagating the Gospel, &c.

1848 to 1866. Member of Executive Committee Society for Relief of Destitute Clergymen.

1828 to 1843. Trustee of Society for Promoting Christian Knowledge, Piety, and Charity.

1843 to 1854. Vice-President of the same.

1854 to 1866. President of the same.

1852 to 1858. President of the Fraternity of Churches.

1853 to 1866. Member for Promoting Theological Education at Cambridge.

18— to 1846. Trustee of the Hopkins Fund.

1835 to 1852. Overseer of Harvard College; and for Fifteen Years Chairman of the Committee for the Examination of Students in Natural Philosophy or Physics.

1861 to 1866. Trustee of the Winthrop Ward Fund in aid of Feeble Unitarian Societies.

All his colleagues agree in acknowledging "the punctuality of his attendance, his deep interest in the objects of the societies with which he was connected, and the wisdom of his counsels and suggestions."

DISCOURSES.

The following Discourses of the Rev. Dr. Barrett have been selected for publication out of the many left behind him, because they are so full of wise, useful, and always timely advice; because they will convey to the reader, as we think, a just and true idea of his general manner and style of discourse in the pulpit; and because they must awaken in the minds of those who sat under his long ministry, into whose hands we hope many of them will fall, associations of the tenderest character, and new and yet stronger feelings of gratitude and reverence.

DISCOURSES.

I.

CHRIST, — HIS NATURE, MISSION, AND CHARACTER.

1 Cor. xi. 3: "I WOULD HAVE YOU KNOW THAT THE HEAD OF EVERY MAN IS CHRIST, AND THE HEAD OF CHRIST IS GOD."

THE subject to which I am to ask your attention this morning is the character of Jesus Christ, — not his moral character, but his official character; a subject involving the long-agitated questions as to his divinity, and the rank he sustains relatively to the great Father of all.

I am aware, as already intimated, that the opinions of nearly all of those who hear me were long ago made up on this topic, and do not, therefore, need for themselves any further discussion of it; but I know also that there are some who are still engaged in the process of investigation, and to whom statements and explanations of our views would be acceptable.

My purpose, then, is to take occasion from the apostle's declaration, "The head of every man is Christ, and the head of Christ is God," to give such an exposition of what liberal Christians generally believe respecting the divinity of the Saviour, as the limits of a single discourse will allow; and to do it with all the explicitness of which I am capable.

I begin with requesting such as are not much accustomed to reading our books on this subject, to fix it in their minds, in the outset, that we make a distinction between Christ's *divinity* and Christ's *deity*. We do not believe in his deity; i.e., we cannot admit that he was God. But we do believe in his divinity. Let me explain.

The expression, "the *deity of Christ*," relates to his *person*, and means that he is God by *nature*. The phrase, "the *divinity* of Christ," may indeed have the same signification; but it may also have a very different one. It may have no relation to his abstract nature and person, but simply to something which he has received from God. Consequently, divinity may be ascribed to him, though, in his nature and person, he is a being distinct from, and inferior to, and dependent upon, the eternal and almighty Father.

In a sense like this, we do ascribe divinity to our Saviour. We would by no means represent him as merely a common man, destitute of every thing superhuman and divine. On the contrary, we believe in, and on all proper occasions would assert, his divinity, according to the just import of the text, and of the Scriptures generally. We have no sympathy with those, if any there be, who delight to degrade the Author and Finisher of our faith below his true rank. No: it is rather our wish and aim to exalt, in our conception, the Son of God, so far as is consistent with the peerless majesty, the absolute supremacy, and the incommunicable glory of the infinite and everlasting Creator, as revealed in the Bible. So far from wishing to take the smallest gem from the crown of our Master, Christ, to shade a single ray of his brightness, or in the least degree to diminish his authority, we long and pray for the happy time when "in the name of Jesus every knee shall bow, and every tongue confess that he is Lord, to the glory of God the Father." To help forward this blessed period, we are anxious that scriptural views of his divinity may be universally diffused and embraced. What, then, is our belief on this all-important subject?

1. First, We believe in the divinity of our Saviour's *mission*. He uniformly declared that he was sent of God; and he proved the truth of his declaration by *doing* what no one could have done, had not God been with him. His language is, "I am come in my Father's name." — "Neither came

I of myself, but he sent me." This was an explicit avowal of a divine mission, and divine we hold it to have really been; but the very idea of his *mission* implies that he had a Superior who could *give* him the mission.

2. Secondly, We believe in the divinity of his *office*. His office as the Messiah is peculiar. He had no predecessor, and will have no successor, in it. It was constituted by God alone. This office, and every thing relating to it, is independent of men, and above all earthly authority. It was established and conferred by the special will of Heaven. Consequently, it is divine; but, obviously, he who was in a condition to *receive* an office could not be the infinite God.

3. Thirdly, We believe in the divinity of his *powers*. "God," saith Scripture, "anointed Jesus of Nazareth with the Holy Spirit and with power." — "He *giveth* not the Spirit by measure unto him." — "He hath *given* him authority, and hath *made* him Lord of all." Without power derived from God in a supernatural way, he could not have been qualified for his divine office, nor fitted to fulfil his divine mission. But one possessed only of *derived* power could not have been himself the Supreme Being.

4. Fourthly, We believe in the divinity of his *doctrine*. What he taught originated with and came from God. He said, "My doctrine is not mine, but His that sent me." — "I have not

spoken of myself; but the Father, who sent me, he gave me commandment what I should say and what I should speak." And the apostles declared the same: "God," said they, "hath in these last days spoken unto us by his Son." Thus, the gospel, as communicated by Jesus Christ, is divine, — divine, not because he himself was Deity, but because the doctrine he taught he received from God.

5. Fifthly, We believe in the divinity of his *works*. Jesus performed miracles, which no unaided man could perform. They were proofs, because effects of supernatural power. He said, "The Father that dwelleth in me, he doeth the works." — "Believe me, that I am in the Father, and the Father in me; or else believe me for the very works' sake." That is, believe me on account of the miracles which it is impossible I should perform without power from on high. Thus, his works were divine, because he was enabled by God to do them; and not because he possessed, in himself, infinite power. His power, as he a hundred times asserted, was obtained from his Father and our Father.

6. Sixthly, We believe in the divinity of that *fulness* which the Scriptures ascribe to him, — fulness of spiritual gifts and blessings, flowing from God through him to the race. He himself was not the source of them; but, as we are told in sacred writ, "it pleased the *Father*, that in him

should all fulness dwell." The inestimable benefits of the gospel which come to us by Jesus Christ could have had their ultimate source in no created being. They are to be traced through the Son of God to God himself, and are the riches of *his* infinite grace. The fulness of the Saviour was divine, not as self-produced, but as supplied by the great and good Being who is above all.

Such, my friends, is the true doctrine of our Saviour's divinity, — the divinity of his *mission*, the divinity of his *office*, the divinity of his *powers*, the divinity of his *doctrines*, the divinity of his *works*, the divinity of the *fulness* that dwelt in him; all, however, in subordination to the absolute supremacy of God the Father.

It is a blessed doctrine. We would cling to it, though all the rest of the world should reject it. It is what makes Christianity valuable to us. We are not the disciples of a *mere* common man. We rely on one who exhibited in all he said and did the marks of divinity. His words and deeds are to us the same, in effect, as the words and deeds of God. What more do we want? What need have we that he should be in his *nature* and *person* the eternal, underived, self-existent One, to whom we pay our highest religious homage?

What do we lose by supposing that he held his divinity in dependence on the Father of all? Is not the light of the sun, that God causes to shine upon us from the sky, just as valuable as it would be if that sun were God himself? Is not the fire that God causes to warm us just as valuable as it would be were that fire God himself? Is not the air which God causes to maintain our life just as valuable as it would be were that air God himself? This no one can deny. Upon the same principle, I ask, are not Jesus Christ and the gospel just as valuable to us as they would be, were either the one or the other, or both, literally and strictly, the infinite and eternal God? What do we lose, by regarding our Saviour, in his *nature* and *person*, as subordinate to the Deity, as the commissioned agent of God's truth and love, while we know that all he said and did are truly divine? We lose nothing; while we save ourselves from numberless perplexities, in which otherwise we should be involved, often as we listened to reason, or read the Scriptures.

1. We lose nothing as to our Saviour's mission. Indeed, it would be a solecism to speak of his mission at all, on the ground that he himself was the Supreme Being. God could not be sent by any one. But Christ was sent; which implies his subordinate rank. Are we deprived of any advantages by this view? Not in the least. Did not he faithfully execute the designs of the Father? Then he is all to us, so far as the gospel is concerned, that the Father himself could have been, had he appeared in his own person.

2. We lose nothing as to his office. Here, again, you perceive the absurdity of the idea that God could be *appointed* to an *office*. But Christ, as the whole New Testament teaches, was so appointed. Do we suffer loss in consequence? By no means. A sovereign's benefaction to his subjects is the same to them, whether conferred by his own hand or by the hand of a subordinate officer. If Jesus performed all the Father's gracious will respecting us, which none deny, then nothing more could have been done, had the Father himself stood visibly on this earth, proclaiming the truths of the gospel, and dying in attestation of them, instead of doing as he chose to do, when he committed these offices to his beloved Son.

3. We lose nothing as to his powers. These are not the less divine, and of course not the less effective for our salvation, because *conferred* on Christ, instead of being *inherently* and *naturally* his. Power is power as much when derived from another as when self-originated. Christ was able to perform miracles, as the Scriptures tell us, because God was with him. Would his miracles have availed any the more, either for his immediate disciples or for us, had he himself been God, and so needed not the aid of a superior Being? Not at all. His powers being, on both suppositions, adequate to the ends for which they were exerted, we derogate from them not the

least by affirming that he received them from the Father.

4. We lose nothing as to his doctrine. Coming from God originally, it is of course divine, by whatever messenger it is borne to us. The deity of Christ's person could not have added any thing to the divinity of his truth. Pure water is pure water, whether we drink it from the spring or from a cup. So, when one brings us glad tidings from the Father of our spirits, it is not so much the nature and rank of the bearer we are concerned with, as it is the message he communicates. Persuade me that the gospel is really a revelation from God, and I value it none the less because it has come through a mediator, instead of having been spoken to man directly from the lips of the Infinite and Eternal One.

5. We lose nothing as to his works. What God does by an agent is the same to us as what he does in his own person. The supernatural works of Jesus have every mark of divinity stamped on them that they would have had if they had been the efforts of the Father Almighty's power acting without any *medium* of exertion.

6. We lose nothing as to his *fulness*, and the blessings communicated by him. This fulness is obviously the same, whether derived or underived. And the blessings brought to us by Christ are as obviously the same, both in nature and value, whether he be a created or uncreated be-

ing. If he is qualified to bring us the means of salvation, these are what chiefly concern us, and not the question, when and where did he begin to exist, or to what order of beings does he belong?

If, then, we find in Christ, God's agent, messenger, and son, every thing we spiritually need, every thing to make us holy and happy, every thing to fill us with the hope of immortal life, what more, I ask again, do we want? Why shall any have misgivings and feel dissatisfied, because they cannot believe that Jesus is himself the Supreme Being? If Christ be qualified for the great duties laid upon him, is it not enough? The personal attributes of Deity cannot be necessary to enable him to perform what God has given him to do, — seeing that the Father is with him and in him. If he be faithful to his trusts, and if he be endued from on high with every fitness to execute the Father's will, what more do we want?

Do we want any thing more to give to the gospel a divine character? Not at all. To constitute the gospel a divine revelation, it was only needful that he who communicated it should have received it from God, should have been commissioned by God to make it known, and should have been empowered by God to give sufficient proof of his divine authority.

Do we want any thing more to assure us of

his being a complete Saviour? Not at all. Is not God himself, according to every view of the subject, the original source of whatever appertains to human salvation? And shall it be said, that his beloved Son, whom he hath sanctified and sent into the world, and on whom he hath poured his Spirit without measure, is still not competent to the work assigned him, not adequate to the office of Saviour, unless he possess, inherently and naturally, all the perfections of the eternal and omnipotent God?

Do we want any thing more to effect the atonement? Not at all. I know that a different feeling exists on this point. It is supposed by some, that, as an infinite Being has been sinned against, the death of an infinite Being was requisite to atone for the sin. But do you not see what this notion leads to? The death of an *infinite* Being, it is said, is necessary; i.e., the death of God himself; for he alone is infinite. At the thought of this, who does not shudder? But, say some Trinitarians, we do not mean that the *divine* part of Christ died: it was only his *human* part. And is it so? Then, I ask, where is the infinite atonement you spoke of? If Christ suffered only in his human nature, infinity is not involved at all in the event of his death. The case being thus, then, whatever the atonement may be supposed to consist in, one *inferior* to the Deity was competent to effect it. One inferior to the Deity *did* effect it. For what says the apostle? "We joy in God through our Lord Jesus Christ, *by* whom we have received the atonement." *By* whom, — I wish you to mark the expression, — *by whom:* this implies *instrumentality.* It shows that Christ was simply the *means* by which the atonement was accomplished. And who was the cause, — who the original mover? Evidently, God. "We joy in *God,*" says the apostle. What does this prove, but that he regarded God as above Jesus, superior to Jesus, and the latter only as the *medium* of God's operations? And what *is* the atonement? Any satisfaction made to the Supreme Being? Evidently not; for he himself is represented as the originator of it. It was the result of his own unchangeable love, insomuch that it was proper for the apostle to *joy in God.* What, then, was it? The word "atonement," you will notice, occurs in no other part of the New Testament; the original Greek word being, in all other cases, translated *reconciliation.* And this is the proper English word: it ought to have been used, instead of "atonement," in the expression just quoted from St. Paul. Yes, reconciliation is the great doctrine of the gospel. To produce reconciliation between God and man was the design of Christ's mission. But, in effecting this reconciliation, which of the parties was to be changed? Not God, but man. For what says the apostle? "We joy in God, through Jesus

Christ, by whom *we* have received the atonement," or, rather, the reconciliation. *We* have received it. Thus man, not God, is the party affected. Jesus is the instrument by which the work is accomplished, and God is the gracious source of the blessing. Is not this view perfectly scriptural, perfectly reasonable too, and perfectly satisfactory? Do you not perceive that the doctrine of the atonement, or reconciliation, does not demand that we suppose Christ to have been the Supreme Being? Nay, is it not utterly incompatible with such a supposition? Is not that sort of divinity which I have ascribed to our Saviour — the divinity of his mission, office, doctrine, works, and the like — all that is necessarily, nay, all that can possibly be, connected with the subject of atonement or reconciliation?

Do we want any thing more in any respect? Not at all. From the induction of particulars to which I have called your attention, you perceive that the supposed deity of Christ is not only without use to Christians, but can rightfully have no connection with it. All we want, and all the gospel record allows, is that kind of divinity which I have described as belonging to our Saviour.

My friends, I have treated the subject in this plain, unadorned, and explicit manner, in order that I might be easily understood by every one; and that our opinions on this important topic, so often discussed among Christians, might not be misapprehended by any. All have, I doubt not, a clear view of the distinction we make between our Saviour's divinity and his deity. He is divine, but he is not God. He is the head of man, but God is the head of Christ.

We shall find satisfaction, I think, in the doctrine I have inculcated, when we approach the communion-table. What would be our emotions, did we come to this ordinance with the belief that we were about to commemorate the death of God? My brothers and sisters, it is with painful feelings that I put such a question; yet it is satisfactory to contemplate the subject occasionally in this light. There are some errors which, to be shunned, need but to be seen in their results. And there are truths which are not duly estimated till they are perceived in contrast with the errors to which they are opposed. Let us be grateful to God that we are free from the appalling views to which I have alluded, and which are still so extensively held. Let us rejoice that we can perform the interesting service of remembrance appointed by our honored Master, without any perplexing and distressing ideas. We can, indeed, find every thing in it to touch the soul, and awaken thoughtfulness and love; but nothing to terrify, nothing to palsy the faculties. It is not the sufferings and death of Deity that we are called on to commemorate; yet there is enough in the thought of our Saviour, as presented in the Gospels, to command our reverence, our affection, and our obedience. His words have, with us, the authority of Heaven. His example is endearing and efficacious, because we believe that it is not too high for us humbly to imitate. His promises of forgiveness excite us to repentance, because we have faith in him as the delegated Messenger of the infinitely merciful God. His death we regard as the seal of his ministry, as a sacrifice called for on account of the sinful state of the world, and as a necessary preliminary step to that glorious resurrection which demonstrated him to be the Son of God, and on which we hang treasures of hope. All this we think sufficient to induce us to honor his memory by obeying his last commandment. My friends, we have been called to be disciples of Jesus: I beseech you, let us be mindful of the privilege. My friends, we have professed to be disciples of Jesus: I beseech you, let us feel our responsibleness, — our responsibleness to Christ as the head of man, and to God as the head of Christ.

II.

THE UNITARIAN CHRISTIAN, IN BELIEF AND PRACTICE.

Eph. iv. 1: "I THEREFORE BESEECH YOU THAT YE WALK WORTHY OF THE VOCATION WHEREWITH YE ARE CALLED."

It seems to me, brethren, that never before have they who claim to be Liberal Christians been in a condition to feel themselves more urgently called upon to be faithful to the trusts confided to them by Providence, than they are at the present day. They who profess to hold the truth of Jesus in freedom and love should now, I think, listen with unaccustomed candor and seriousness to suggestions regarding the great duty of walking worthily of their vocation; i.e., of acting up to their principles. This is an obligation of the first moment always: it is especially so in times like these, when many deceptive lights glimmer on either hand to betray the unsuspecting into wrong courses; when the atmosphere of religion is surcharged with impure and dangerous elements; and when the doubting and weary hesitate to adopt any of the multiplied forms of Christianity, till they have the opportunity of seeing a more favorable exemplification of its principles in practice. To distinguish the superficial and specious from the true and substantial, is an exercise of discrimination to which nothing will so effectually help the mass of our fellow-men as a manifest correspondence between professed belief and actual conduct on the part of those whose intelligence and sound position give them influence in the community. Liberal Christians, so called, suppose themselves — and I doubt not justly — to be in possession of the simple, pure, and saving truths of the primitive gospel; to have and to hold the faith taught and exemplified by the Son of God, free from the additions it received in its passage through the dark ages: and they are also heard to declare, often and in earnest tones, that they desire no other thing so much as the universal prevalence of those truths and of that faith. Now, the case being so, and it being at the same time clear that in no other way can right sentiments in religion be so effectually diffused as by a full practical exhibition of them in the lives of their friends and advocates, what — the question presents itself naturally and forcibly — what can be more incumbent on this class of Christ's followers than the duty of maintaining a strict consistency between what they believe and say, and what they are and do; between the faith they profess and the conduct they manifest; between the manner of persons they contemplate in theory, and the manner of persons they seek to become in character?

And here let me suggest, in passing, that they who rank themselves among Liberal Christians ought by no means to rest content with being about as good as others of a less pure and enlightened faith. A great deal better, most certainly, they should be; and they would be a great deal better, if they did but act up to their principles. Many, to a considerable degree, do so; and these exhibit superior elevation, dignity, and beauty of character. Some, however, I am sorry to say, do not thus act up to their principles; their conduct is unworthy of their creed; they dishonor the name they have assumed; they bring discredit upon the cause they profess to expound. Do any here present belong to this number? I hope not. But let us all look into our hearts and upon our lives; let us compare what we are and do with what we believe and affirm; and then let us answer the question, — as to whether we walk worthily of our vocation, — each one for himself, to his conscience and his God.

My hearers, it is one of the chief glories of what is termed Liberal Christianity, that its standard of character is exceedingly elevated, and that all its distinctive principles have the effect, when carried out in practice, to advance its disciples in the best way of moral and religious excellence. Unlike some systems of theology that have prevailed, it has nothing in it to perplex, depress, or discourage; but every thing to animate, every thing to lift up and carry forward those who heartily embrace its truths, and strive, with the strength God gives them, to walk worthily of their vocation. Would any, especially of the younger class of my auditors, have this shown?

1. First, then, consider our views of human nature. Can any be conceived of more ennobling? —any better suited to raise and perfect the character? In the degrading fiction of hereditary total depravity we have no belief: the paralyzing dogma of entire moral impotency we reject. In place of these, we adopt the encouraging, elevating truths, that man comes from his Creator's hand innocent and well made, and capable, with the assistance God continually vouchsafes, to do his duty; that the Author of his being and the Disposer of his lot has given him, not only the ability, but also the means, requisite for working out his salvation; and that as he now uses both the one and the other, so will be his condition hereafter. Now, can any one fail to perceive the superior practical advantage that such views have over the opposite theory, which, while it asserts the entire corruption of man's nature, denies to him the power either to think a good thought or to perform a good deed?

Apply the leading principle they involve to secular matters, and see how it must operate there. Convince the agriculturist, for example, while sitting in his house on a summer's morning, that he is sick from head to foot, and cannot work to any purpose, if he should go out into his field: will he, in consequence, be any the more likely, do you think, to get up and direct his way thither? Persuade your son, before he goes to school, that he is a dunce, that he has no aptitude, no natural ability, for learning, and will he then, can you suppose, have much heart for study? Just so as regards morals and religion: settle it in the minds of men, that they are, by nature, totally depraved, and of course altogether impotent for virtue and piety, and what reason can you have to expect that they will set about the *practice* of piety and virtue? But how different ought the case to be where correct views prevail! There men know and feel, that, through the goodness of Him who created them in his own image, they have the capacity and the power for high attainments; and the only thing wanting is, that they be persuaded to make good use of this capacity and this power.

Is it true, then, my hearers, and do we believe it, that there is within us a divine, immortal principle; that the inspiration of the Almighty hath given us understanding; that the faculties God has bestowed on us are adequate to the performance of the duties he requires of us; and, if faithful to our trusts, we shall hereafter be placed in far wider and happier spheres of exertion? What, therefore, ought not to be expected of us? What gratitude to the great and good Being who has so richly endued us? What careful heed to our ways, lest we ill requite him, and subject ourselves to shame by the abuse of our power? What dread of every thing mean and low and sinful? What aspirations after excellence? What endeavors to walk worthily of our high vocation?

2. Advert, secondly, to the manner in which we are accustomed to think and speak of God. Nothing revolts us more than the views some Christians have entertained of the Deity. Why, my hearers, you know as well as I — for you are not unacquainted with erroneous systems of theology — that certain attributes have been ascribed to the Supreme Being, which, did they belong to any man in your neighborhood, you would fly from him with horror. But I will not now describe them; rather let me hasten to remind you of the sentiments of Liberal Christians respecting God. Can any be so delightful, so winning, as these? How do we regard this great and good Being? Do we not look up to him as to our Father? Do we not believe that all our thoughts and feelings relating to him ought to be, in the best sense of the term, filial? Do we not say that we are his children; that we are loved, provided for, and blessed by him continually; and that we expect

no other treatment from him, either in the present or future life, than what is perfectly consistent with parental wisdom and goodness? Yes; and we joy in these convictions, these feelings, these hopes. We would not exchange them for the wealth of worlds. So far, very well; but is this all? What — I appeal to ingenuous minds — what manner of persons ought we not to be in practical piety? Should we be content with a common share of this virtue? Ought not something more of this essential quality of character to be expected of us than has generally prevailed in the world? Should we not live nearer to God, find more delight in communion with him, converse about him oftener and with greater satisfaction, and render him a more willing, affectionate, unreserved obedience, than they do or can who were educated under the old scheme of election and reprobation, and its associated dogmas? Most certainly, this is but our reasonable service; and I beseech you by the mercies of God, let us render it; let us show, by our conduct, that it is not in vain that we have more correct views of the divine character and government than others; let us see to it, that we grow every day less and less insensible to our heavenly Father's presence, less indifferent to the marks of his goodness, less cold in our devotions, less reluctant to speak of his loving-kindness and tender mercies, less sluggish in performing the duties he has enjoined, and so to walk worthily of the vocation wherewith we are called.

3. Think, in the third place, of the light in which we view Jesus Christ. How clear, how cheerful, how quickening, it is! How unlike the medium through which he has been seen by multitudes! We regard him, not as the infinite and eternal God himself, but as his beloved Son, and therefore as one with whom we can sympathize, and whom we may attempt to imitate, with the hope of making some approaches towards the standard of his virtues; as one who has walked our earth, and lived amongst men, and found, by experience, what are the trials and duties of humanity; as one who not only taught how we should act, but gave us a pattern in his own conduct; who, not content with pointing out the way we should tread, trod it himself. Yes, brethren, and consequently how near and familiar he seems to us! how practicable the divine law appears, now that we see it carried out in actual conduct before us! Yes, we perceive how he was tried, how he strove, how he triumphed; and in this we have at once an example and a motive. All the dispositions we are invited to cherish, he cherished; all the virtues we are called upon to practise, he practised; the complete character we are bidden to form, he formed. Our model is before us; our instruments are put into our hands; our work we are shown, both by word

and by hand, how to execute; and our reward, as was his, is in the heavens. Far otherwise would the case be with us, were we forced to behold in Jesus the eternal, self-existent, infinite Jehovah; and perplexed, withal, by the other strange and contradictory doctrines connected with that theory. Who does not at once discern the superiority of such views respecting the Saviour, especially as regards their influence on human motives and conduct, over others that have prevailed in the Church? They are all simple, easily understood, accordant with the dictates of reason, obviously the only ones sustained by the current language of Scripture, and entirely practical. *Practical*, I say; and I beg you to observe how manifestly the fact is so, by adverting, for one moment, to a point which Calvinism sets prominently forth, as if it were of the utmost importance; and yet how such a speculation can exert any good influence on human motive and conduct, it would puzzle a plain, unsophisticated mind to conceive. I refer to the great object of Christ's mission, which the dark theology above named affirms, among other incredible things, to have been, that he might suffer, as a substitute for our totally depraved race or the elect portions of it, the full amount of punishment incurred by them through Adam's fall and their own trans gressions, that so God might be enabled or induced to treat them with favor. Not thus, however, does the theology of Liberal Christians and of the Bible teach. What, according to them, was the leading object of Christ's mission? As I proceed to answer the question in a few words, my hearers will notice how all he was commissioned to do and suffer has a practical bearing on man's character and conduct. Christ came into the world, then, not, as Calvinism asserts, to quench God's wrath; not to satisfy divine justice; not to cancel the demands of the moral law on our race; not to supply man's deficiencies by a substitution of his own obedience; not to suffer, in his own innocent person, the punishment due to Adam, and the myriads of our race after him, for their depravity: but he came for other purposes, — purposes worthy of the character and government of the wise and beneficent Father who sent him; he came to deliver us from our own vices, instead of having to do with the sin of our first progenitor; he came to make us do our own duty, instead of performing that duty for us; he came to induce us to obey the law, instead of answering the claims of that law himself; he came to prompt us to personal obedience, instead of putting his obedience in the place of our own; he came to quench the fire of bad passion burning within ourselves, instead of that of God's anger; he came to enthrone the principles of justice in human hearts, instead of satisfying the divine justice; he came to win us to our Heavenly Father, who is, and always was, ready to pardon the returning sinner, instead of altering the mind of Deity by paying him an equivalent for man's transgression; he came, in fine, to destroy the kingdom of evil within us, and to establish there the kingdom of good, by giving us a religion replete with directions, motives, and all needed assistances, whereby we might subdue the power of sin, eradicate false sentiments, be filled with love to God, with love to man, with all fit desires of duty, and thus to put us in the way of working out our own salvation. This, this, is what our blessed Saviour came for. All that he did and suffered was designed to operate, not on God, but on mankind; all was intended to help men to become holy, that they might be happy. How reasonable as well as scriptural, how beautiful, how worthy of the beneficent Father above, how useful to his children, does not all this seem! Who does not perceive in this, as in other respects, the advantage of our views over doctrines that have for ages been the burden of human creeds and catechisms?

Practical, I say; and, I beseech you, let not the advantage be lost upon us. Let it not be in vain for us, that we see in Jesus, and in his divine religion, so much to animate and encourage us; that we find every thing pertaining to his character and labors and sufferings intended and suited to have a direct bearing on our own minds, hearts, and lives. Oh, shame, shame on us, if, with such views, our Saviour is not loved and obeyed by us; if he does not take strong hold on our sympathies; if he does not draw us after him with a force and uniformity unknown where a false theology prevails; if, with such a vocation as ours, we do not strive, with a zeal and constancy like that of the primitive disciples, to walk worthily of it!

4. How beautiful, we say, in the fourth place, is our theory of Christian charity! What is it? That no good person shall be excluded from our love for honest difference of opinion; no faithful seeker after truth condemned for conclusions he could not help arriving at; no one treated with unkindness for choosing, in the fair exercise of his freedom and judgment, a faith, church, or sect different from our own: but that all, of whatever name or party, who believe in Christ and aim to obey him, ought to be regarded as brethren, and esteemed according to their moral worth. Can any thing, we ask, be better than this? Let such a law of mutual respect, affection, and behavior prevail, and there would be something of heaven itself on earth. Who can contemplate thus our theory of Christian charity, without being enamoured with it? But theory, brethren, is of little avail, except it be reduced to practice. No doubt, Liberal Christians

in general are really, as well as professedly, more charitable than others. From their churches no good person is excluded on account of mere difference of opinion: wherever their principles have sway, individuals are not subjected to persecution for not agreeing with the majority on the disputed points of controversial theology. All enjoy freedom of thought and of speech; and the only qualifications deemed essential for full communion in the bonds of Christianity are a sincerely good heart and a truly virtuous life, growing out of faith in God and his Son Jesus Christ. Still, notwithstanding the general practice, among Liberal Christians, of these principles of an enlarged charity which they profess, there are doubtless some exceptions. How is it with us? permit me to ask again. I judge no man; but it is mine to beseech you that ye walk worthily of the vocation with which ye are called. I conjure all who are liberal in theory, to be liberal in practice, and to maintain a strict correspondence between the charity they profess and the charity they exercise. Common consistency puts in no less a claim than this; and this — who does not know? — Christ himself has made one of the tests of discipleship.

5. Again, my hearers, what is our habit of thinking and speaking of the Holy Scriptures and of human creeds? The latter we hold to be worthless or worse; the former, as above all price.

The Bible, the Bible, we say, is our rule of faith and conduct. To others we leave the formularies of men's devising: as for ourselves, no writings shall even seem to stand upon equal footing with those of the sacred volume. Here is the charter of our privileges; here the sure guide to the whole duty of man. What to us are human creeds and confessions, and decrees of popes, bishops, synods, and councils, while we have in our hands this precious book, this full expression of the mind of God respecting his children, this sufficient treasury of divine truth touching our origin, our nature, our duty, and our destination? We want no more than this. The Bible, with the reason God has given us to interpret and apply it, we hold to be enough. To the law and the testimony, not to catechisms and covenants which man's ingenuity has contrived, do we choose to recur in all matters of religious doubt and difficulty. So we say, and we say well. But let us not forget, brethren, that there is something to be done as well as said. How are we using this holy volume, which we profess to value so highly? My brother, art thou a Liberal Christian? and dost thou, after all thy declared respect for the Sacred Scriptures as the authoritative standard in matters of faith and practice, neglect them? Is this blessed book seen on thy shelf covered over with the dust of many months? Then let me say to thee, in all plainness of speech, thou art but a poor representative of the class of Christians to which thou belongest. Thy conduct gives the lie to thy profession. Thine inconsistency is disgraceful. It is worse: thyself art injured by it; thy brethren in the faith are saddened; and the cause of Christ and of God is prejudiced by it. I beseech thee, change thy practice; make it accord with thy principles; and henceforth, in this respect as in others, walk worthily of the vocation wherewith thou art called.

6. Take, finally, the views we cherish of the great law of future recompense. We think them scriptural and rational; and we believe they afford the strongest dissuasives from sin, and the most powerful inducements to holiness. While with unutterable horror we turn from the Calvinist doctrine of everlasting hell-torments, and while we reject all theories of arbitrary, vindictive dispensations of rewards and punishment under the divine government, we hold that there is a connection between vice and misery, and between virtue and happiness, as natural and indissoluble as that which belongs to any class of causes and effects. In other words, the bad man does or will suffer in proportion to his badness, and the good man does or will enjoy in proportion to his goodness, as certainly and as accordantly with the established principles of Nature and Providence, as a living seed, put into the warm, moist earth,

does or will vegetate. Nor is this law, as we believe, restricted in its operation exclusively either to the present or to the future world. It belongs to both worlds. The dissolution of the body may modify some of its results, but will not essentially alter the character of them. We hold that this life and the next is one continuous state of existence, so that all which is strictly ourself here, will be ourself there. Death we look upon only as a brief passage-way from the one to the other, through which the soul is but a moment, as it were, in going; carrying with it all its habits of thought and feeling, all its capacities, tastes, and preferences, — all, in a word, of virtue and happiness, or of vice and misery, — it commenced in this introductory state of its being. Can any views be more reasonable, or more scriptural, or more effective for holiness, than these? When, under the full impression of the truth of such doctrine, we listen to the exhortation, "Walk worthily of your high vocation," who of us can remain indifferent? who unmoved? How much has the sinner, who repents not, to fear! How much has the virtuous man to hope for! O brethren! let us bring this subject close home to our inmost soul. What! is it a fact, supported alike by reason and revelation, and have we not the least doubt of it, that misery is bound to vice, and happiness to virtue, by ties which neither time nor death will sever; that there is a law of just recompense, whose operation nothing can long counteract; that as we sow we shall sooner or later reap; that we must enter on the future life with the same intellectual and moral qualities with which we leave the present; and that our condition there will correspond, at any given period, with the character we possess at that period, — is all this true, and do we believe it? What manner of persons, then, ought we to be? What purity, what intelligence, what holiness, what efforts for every virtue and every grace that can ennoble and adorn our nature, should not distinguish us?

My hearers, I might pursue this subject much further. It would be easy to show, that all the distinctive articles of our faith, all our leading principles, have, in point of simplicity, reasonableness, scriptural authority, harmony, power, and beauty, peculiar and great practical advantages; and that, on the equitable ground that from them to whom much is given much is required, we, as a class of Christians, ought to be better, a great deal better, than others.

But I have already gone sufficiently into detail. It remains to me only, in conclusion, to present a brief sketch of the sort of character we should not fail, each and all of us, to exhibit, if we did but walk worthily of our vocation; if we were disposed, at all times and in all places, to act up to the principles of our profession, as stated in the foregoing discourse. What is this character?

First, It is that of one who, considering his nature a good nature, the gift of God, and a treasure of unspeakable value, is thankful for it, takes care of it, respects it, speaks well of it, cultivates its capacities and powers, shuns whatever can sully its brightness, and seeks association with every thing that can help to improve, ennoble, and adorn it.

Secondly, It is that of one who habitually looks up to God as to a Father and Friend; loves the Being upon whom he is so dependent, and to whom he is so much indebted; delights to hold communion with him; and aims to have his actions and temper agree, in all respects, with the divine will.

Thirdly, It is that of one who, regarding Jesus Christ as God's chosen Son, sent for the good of man, directs his thoughts towards this wise and gracious Saviour with love and gratitude; and, while he admires the truth he taught and the example he left to his followers, obeys the one, and imitates the other.

Fourthly, It is that of one who is full of charity; who abounds in affectionate regards for his neighbor; who cherishes, always and everywhere, kind feelings towards, not only those who agree with him in opinion, but those also who differ; and who avails himself of all fit opportunities for doing good to his fellow-men.

Fifthly, It is that of one who, while he respects and reverences the records of divine revelation contained in the Bible, is a constant reader of them ; who deems it alike a privilege and a duty to recur to them for guidance, motive, and consolation ; and who, animated by the holy spirit they breathe, strives to act by the great moral rules they teach, in daily practice.

Finally, It is that of one who, knowing that he lives not for the present alone, but also for the future, provides for the coming ages, by forming habits of thought, feeling, and conduct, that will make him happy when the flesh decays and falls off, and when the immortal mind, released from the body and removed from this material world, must depend, for joy and hope, on resources within itself, and on those spiritual fountains of bliss to which the pure and virtuous soul alone can have access.

Such, my hearers, if I understand the subject, is that sort of character which is exhibited by the Liberal Christian who walks worthily of the vocation wherewith he is called. Can there be an individual here, having the heart of a human being in him, that does not approve and desire to possess this character ? Who, if wise, would not sacrifice any worldly good for its attainment? How sublime, how beautiful, beyond expression, is such an example of cultivated, sanctified, perfected human nature! It is every thing we were created to be; every thing we should pray and strive to become; every thing that can secure respect, love, joy, and hope on earth; and every thing that fits for honor, glory, and happiness in heaven.

God grant that here, under the continued ministrations of a rational and scriptural Christianity, specimens of such a character may abound, for the glory of the Father of all and his blessed Son, for the present and future welfare of this community, and for the credit and furtherance of the incorrupt gospel in the world!

III.

MAN'S ABILITY THE MEASURE OF HIS DUTY.

Matt. xxv. 15: "EVERY MAN ACCORDING TO HIS SEVERAL ABILITY."

WE have here a point to which I wish to call your attention this afternoon. It is, that every one is *able* to do what God *requires* of every one; or, in other words, God looks to us for that, and only that, which he has given us the ability to render. He who receives ten talents is responsible for ten; he who has five, for five; and he who has but one, for only this one. The subject, if I mistake not, is one of great practical importance. Our ability is the measure of our duty. We *can* do all that our Heavenly Father demands of us; and the question, often as he shall call us to account, will be, "Have we done what we were able to do?"

I repeat: *We can* do *all* that God requires of us. In stating this proposition, rational and scriptural as it is, I oppose a prevalent notion, encouraged for ages by false theologies,—which is this: that, in our spiritual concerns, we can do little or nothing for ourselves; or, in other words, that to say we have done what we were able, though we say it ever so truly, will not avail to our acceptance with God. Those false theologies, which rule many minds even in our day, assert, that all the strivings of any man to be good, all the works of righteousness which any man can perform, amount to just nothing in respect to his salvation, unless he was chosen thereunto from the foundation of the world; unless he has been regenerated or made over again by supernatural power; and unless he has a certain view of, or faith in, one atonement, whereby the merits of another can be put to his own credit. Or, to express the theory in different language, the great and good Being whom we call our Father in heaven will never approve, accept, and bless his children, either for their intrinsic goodness or for the good they themselves have done, but only on account, or for the sake, of some outside considerations, such as the decree of election, and the operation of the Holy Ghost, and the vicarious death of the second person of a triune God.

Now, brethren, such a statement of doctrine as this may seem very strange to us; and some may doubt whether anybody ever believed it. But history informs us, that, during long centuries, it was the creed of a vast majority of Christians; and it is, at this hour, to be found among the written formularies of faith in thousands of churches. And though we may fancy that it has nearly died out in our neighborhood, yet its influence is still very extensively felt. For though most intelligent and reflecting persons do not fall into the extreme of supposing that the qualifications for divine favor can be obtained in the arbitrary manner above indicated, yet there is, nevertheless, a confused notion, very prevalent, that religion is a sort of thing by itself; and that a habit of piety, acceptable to God, is different in its nature, origin, and progress, from all other acquired habits and affections of the mind: so that the same principles and rules which apply to the formation, discipline, and improvement of the one, are not equally applicable to the other; or, in other words, that for one to be able to say he has done what he was able is not enough for his salvation, unless he happens, at the same time, to believe in the doctrines of grace, as they are called, to which reference has just been made.

Now, I take it upon me to assert, that the theological theory adverted to is not only false, but that it has been the nurse of many speculative errors, and, what is worse, of many mischievous practical consequences; for example, —

1. It has led superficial thinkers to combine the idea of something mysterious, unintelligible, and impracticable with religion; giving multi-

tudes the impression, that Christianity is either irrational and contradictory to the laws of human nature, or incapable of being reduced to practice by human exertions: and thus it has served as pretext for scepticism.

2. It has also been a source of much anxiety and uneasiness to many truly serious and upright minds, and has deprived them of the satisfaction to which they were entitled from the consciousness of general integrity, by leading them to imagine that something else was necessary to secure the favor of God, beside a faithful performance of every known duty; and, not having any distinct notion what this something was, they have been tormented with groundless apprehensions, lest they might be found deficient in that which the Judge of all would deem essential to their salvation.

3. Again, it has led not a few into errors still more harmful, by inducing them to substitute something foreign to the true nature of religion, or at least something that is merely accidental to it, or perhaps a single branch of it, for the whole of Christian duty, which implies the uniform and daily practice of virtue and piety; so that, while a disproportionate attention has been paid to the circumstantials of religion, a total neglect has prevailed in many quarters as to those *moral habits* which are of vital importance. Thus, some have placed the essence of religion

in a warm attachment to articles of belief, and have hoped to deserve heaven by untiring sectarian zeal for prescribed creeds. Others have imagined their religion to be most acceptable to God, and best fitted to secure them salvation, when it was concerned in the greatest degree possible with outward ceremonies, such as fasts and penances, and all sorts of ritual observances. Still another class, by no means small, have supposed that their religion, in order to its being in the largest measure well pleasing in the divine sight, must consist in *ecstasies* of feeling, in *raptures* of pious sentiment; which, however, as all thoughtful observers know, depend often and very much upon the state of the animal spirits and bodily health; which are frequently experienced by persons of little deeply seated religious principle, but of irritable tempers; and to which many conscientious people, who strive every hour to do their duty, but whose natural feelings are less excitable, are entire strangers. Others, again, have fancied that they were in the safest way to heaven when thinking and speaking most disparagingly of human nature, and most extravagantly of God's sovereign grace in the conversion of sinners; and when, in accordance with this mode of thought and speech, they were rendering themselves as *passive* as possible, and as *dependent* as it was in their power to do upon special divine influences from above. Ask persons of this sort why they are not good, practical Christians, and they are ready to say, "Oh, this vile nature of ours!" — "How *can* we do any thing of ourselves?" Ask them again, and the answer may be, that "God has not yet seen fit to convert us." — "We are waiting for the regenerating influences of the Holy Spirit." Thus, the false notion which I have before alluded to is made the apology for positive disobedience, or at least for useless inactivity. Now, it has often seemed to me, that this erroneous idea is a cause of more spiritual inaction, and is therefore more hostile to Christian improvement, than most of the other speculative errors in theology which have found currency in the world. As far as it is practically cherished, it renders powerless the noblest and most effective motives to virtue. Religion, in this view, becomes the foe, instead of the friend, of morality. Convince a boy that he can do nothing towards getting a living, and that his father is able and willing to do every thing, and what have you done but put a notion in his head that will tend to make him lazy and inefficient? So, persuade men that they are by nature impotent for good, and God is the only agent in their salvation, and do you not thereby lessen their inducement to work for themselves?

4. There is still another class of people, who, instead of doing what they are able, — instead of

looking upon the gospel as a system of means and motives, whereby they may, if they please, work out their own salvation, — are in the habit of making their religion consist in a sort of *inactive* love of Christ; in committing themselves to Christ; in throwing themselves into the arms of Christ, as some express it; in relying on him *alone* for salvation; in trusting wholly in his mediation and atonement for their acceptance with God. Let me not be misunderstood. In such a regard for Christ, and for what he hath done for mankind, as he taught his followers to cherish, is most certainly to be found every one's high interest and bounden duty. But the fault of the persons to whom I refer is, that theirs is an *inactive* regard. It is a dependence on what has been done *for* them that prevents them doing what they are able for themselves. Whereas, they ought to remember, that all which Jesus has done *for* them, indescribably great as are his benefactions, will be in vain, so far as they are concerned, unless they turn these benefactions of his to a practical use; i.e., unless they make them the means and motives of active obedience to God's moral law. And this statement agrees with the words of the Saviour himself: "He that hath my commandments, and *keepeth* them, he it is that loveth me." It agrees, too, with the whole tenor of the New Testament. In a word, Scripture and reason agree in teaching that every man has a work to do himself; that Christ has done nothing which will benefit *him* whose presumptuous reliance on the Saviour's merits, whatever those may be, is thought sufficient to excuse him from laboring to acquire virtue of his own. "She hath done what she could." This, you remember, was what called forth the benediction of Jesus on one of the Marys; and not the application, on the part of the woman, of Christ's righteousness to make up her deficiencies. Indeed, the application of Christ's righteousness to ourselves, though a common expression in theological formularies, is a phrase altogether unscriptural and absurd. Righteousness is personal: no one can give it to another. True, the righteousness of the Son of God was perfect; but no direct transfer of a particle of it can be made to us. The only way we can be profited by Christ's righteousness is by making it our pattern; or by so using his truth, his will, his whole religion, that we may work out a righteousness of our own, like his in quality, if not in measure.

I have spoken of some of the speculative errors and mischievous practical consequences which flow from the false notion, that something more than doing what we are able is necessary to ensure the favor of God. There are many others that might be mentioned; but I pass them by unnoticed, that I may suggest a few considerations, adapted to strengthen our confidence in the fact, that we have the ability, all and each of us, to do every thing that God requires of us, every thing that is necessary to our salvation. And here it is difficult for me entirely to suppress the feeling that I undertake to prove what is self-evident to every mind. But I correct myself. I must not forget the immense power of education, and the prevalence of false maxims in a community, to bias and darken the youthful mind, so as to render it incapable, in mature years, of discerning accurately what else it might apprehend with perfect ease and correctness. It has been so long customary to look upon human nature as a mass of moral corruption and utter helplessness, and to pervert the meaning of certain scriptural expressions, — such as "called," "converted," "regenerated," and the like, — so as to make them express a supposed supernatural change, which, according to the popular system, takes place from a state of nature to a state of grace in those who are elected by the sovereign pleasure of God from the rest of the world, — that religion has come to be regarded as something totally different in its nature, origin, and progress, from every other habit and affection; as something that bears no analogy to any other human acquisition, either in its source or in its growth; as something, in fine, which, instead of being acquired by the use of natural and efficient means, in the way of mental and moral habits, is wholly an extrinsic quality, and superintended by a foreign and miraculous influence, and is only to be found in those who, by special favor, are chosen to salvation. The case being so, my friends, there may be occasion for trying to prove what else it would be lost labor to attempt.

I proceed, then, to say, that there is a sense in which every pious heart feels the maxim, "We can do nothing of ourselves," to be perfectly true, and of the highest importance. When we mean by it that all our powers of body and mind are originally the gift of God; that it is his ever-present energy that continues and supports them; that, if his influence were withdrawn, our strength would instantly be dissolved into more than infant weakness, and the loftiest human faculties would be unequal to the smallest exertion, — we say no more than all reason and all Scripture justify and confirm. But the fullest conviction of the truth, that we can do nothing *originally* of ourselves and independently of the sustaining power of the Deity, is consistent with the belief, that *we can do all that God has given us the ability to do;* so that, in an important sense, — nay, in every practical sense, — you perceive it would be a falsehood to say we can do nothing. Has God given me the power to stretch out my hand? — then it would be false to say I cannot stretch it out. Has God given me the power to exert certain intellectual faculties, such as reason, memory, and judgment? — then it would be false to say I cannot exert them. Has God given me the power to choose between good and evil, right and wrong, and also the power of securing the one and avoiding the other? — then it would be false to say I cannot exercise these powers. In a word, has God, by what he has done, given me the ability to work out my own salvation? — then it is false to say that I cannot work it out.

Now I take another step, and, instead of speaking hypothetically, state positively, that God has given to each and all of us the ability to work out our own salvation, just as much, and precisely in the same sense, that he has given us the power to stretch out our hand, to use the faculties of reason, memory, and judgment, and to choose between good and evil; or, in other words, that religion, or, if you please, salvation, is exactly as much dependent upon our own will and exertion for its attainment, as any of our other affections, habits, or possessions. Were it not so, why are we addressed in the Scriptures as free agents, capable of moral endeavor, responsible for our actions, and destined to punishment or reward, according to our doings and character? Indeed, every page of the Bible, unless its language be misinterpreted, bears testimony to this position. The known character of God bears testimony to it. Our own reason bears testimony to it. Our experience bears testimony to it. Every thing bears testimony to the fact that we have the ability to do what our Maker requires of us; or, in other words, to perform our duty; or, in still different language, to work out our own salvation. This is a conclusion of great practical moment: for only convince a man that he is unable to do any thing, and he will not be apt to attempt any thing; but, on the other hand, make him know and feel that he *can* do much, and you may expect that he will bestir himself at once, and with an energy promising success. How important, then, that Christian teachers stop ringing all manner of changes on the old dogma of man's utter impotency, and that they set forth clearly and forcibly the great, quickening truth, that all, under God, can be good and happy, if they will but exert themselves!

I now advance one step further, and say, not only that we have the power to do what God requires of us,— to work out our own salvation,— but also that we shall be judged by the comparison of what we have done with what we could do. The man who had received the one talent was condemned because he did not use the ability he possessed to make it productive. And this is the universal rule of the divine procedure. God requires of none of his creatures what it is impossible for them to render. He only demands of them the service which he has given them the ability to perform. They who wish well and do all they can for their fellow-men, are just as worthy, in the eye of Heaven, as they who, having greater means, do more. Yes, it is doing well according to our ability that qualifies us for God's favor. If every other testimony were silent, the scriptural representation of the final judgment would establish this position. The one inquiry on that solemn occasion will be, Have ye done what ye were able to do? "Not every one that saith unto me, Lord, Lord, shall enter the kingdom, but he that doeth the will of my Father." And what is this will of the Father? It is that every one do as much as he can. This all-important truth is sufficiently taught, to say nothing of other passages of Scripture, in the parable of the talents. He who had ten was required to render ten; he who had five, to render five; and he who had one was rejected, because he did not make a corresponding return, — did not do what he was able, — but went and buried the talent in the earth.

My friends, many important practical inferences may be derived from the subject. 1. First, It affords encouragement to all to enter upon a course of virtuous conduct. The rewards of virtue are not confined to men of the greatest ability. Every one will be recompensed according to what he does, be his ability ever so small. We have all, therefore, whether high or low, rich or poor, powerful or weak, learned or ignorant, equal encouragement, so far as relates to divine acceptance, to cultivate a virtuous temper and live a virtuous life.

2. Secondly, It suggests consolation to those who have failed in their well-meant endeavors. Do you, benefactor of men, — do you sigh that your efforts to do good are so often in vain; that you find yourself so frequently crossed by the malevolence of the wicked, or the mistaken sentiments and incorrigible prejudices of the weak? and, when you sit down after the fervent but ineffectual struggle, do you feel your heart sicken within you? I bid you be of good courage, and console yourself with the thought that you have done what you were able, and that Heaven sees your sincerity, and will reward your well-meant though unsuccessful endeavors.

3. Again, our subject should lead us to look round with love and respect upon all honest and good men, however confined in their sphere of usefulness. There is nothing contemptible in natural weakness. They who do all they can are approved of God: let us approve them too. We must not judge the world by what is done alone, but by this in connection with the *ability* there is of doing. There is much effort that we

do not see, much that is not crowned with success. There is kindness, whose gifts are scanty on account of limited means of bestowing. The poor have many friends that cannot feed them; many that must content themselves with a friend's feelings, without being able to put bread into their mouths. But they have done what they were able, and *are* doing what they can; and let *us* look upon them with the favoring eye with which Jesus beheld the indigent woman who cast into the treasury her single mite, which was all she had.

4. But, in the last place, let us not forget that certainly we are called upon to do all which we are able. Less than this will not answer the demand of God, nor satisfy our own consciences. There is no substitute for our voluntary deficiencies. We must suffer in exact proportion as we fall short of what we have the ability to perform. I pray you, then, to act up to the capacities and powers of your nature, and the privileges and opportunities you enjoy; and take that course through life which alone can recommend you to God, and secure for you the happiness promised to the virtuous.

IV.

THE CHRISTIAN LIFE.

COMMAND TO WORK. — TIME. — SPHERE OF ACTION.

Matt. xxi. 28: "SON, GO WORK TO-DAY IN MY VINEYARD."

THE coming of a new year is hailed by different hearts with strangely differing emotions, — by many with longings, by some with dread, by others with dull and thoughtless unconcern. There are many who look back with sorrow on the old year's wasted track, its neglected harvests of good, its follies, and its irrevocable departure; many, too, children of distress, who give thanks in pain and sorrow, that it is gone, that a part of the long burden of suffering is lifted away. There are more, greeting joyfully, without a shadow on their hopes, the advent of the new, — its fair promises of success, the prize in its right hand, of improvement and honor. But to all these may be one and the same resolve, — to study and to obey the great discipline which the year shall surely bring; to hearken for it, to watch for it, and to heed it; to make this a new year indeed, — new in a more unremitting diligence, a more self-sacrificing benevolence, a purer devotion, and a braver heroism. "He is in the way of life," saith the Scripture, — in the true and peaceful way of life, — "who keepeth" in his heart and in his deeds its rich and hallowed "instruction." That to all the new year may be happy, and yet rather that it may be virtuous, — that it may be happy by being virtuous, by being crowned with disinterested sentiments, noble thoughts, and honorable works; and that it may be held long in their grateful remembrance by the part it shall have borne in maturing their souls into a Christian excellence, — is the fervent wish of the preacher.

But the text, "Go work to-day in my vineyard." Go *work:* here is a call to action, — a call in the gospel from God to every human being; and to it there is something to respond in our nature. We feel that to work ought to be, as it is, our vocation; and Christianity does not, like some creeds of men's device, contradict this sentiment. Christianity does not rebuke our energies. It does not repress or paralyze the self-helping activity of the manliest heart amongst us. It does not mock and tantalize us, by telling us that we can do nothing of ourselves, that we are helpless, that the power is taken out of our hands, that hereditary sin has shorn us of our strength before we had begun to exercise it, and that Adam put fetters on our moral faculties before we were born. It does not tell us, like the Assembly's Catechism, that we can do nothing except evil; but, contrariwise, that, exposed and frail and tempted and yielding as our moral nature is, it has nevertheless the seeds of great harvests, and the elements of mighty struggles, and the capacity of noble resistance, and the guaranty of final triumph in it. It does not smite us into flat dejection by telling us we can do nothing: it assures us, and by all solemn warnings bids us hearken to the assurance, that through Christ and God, whom we are sure to find by seeking, we can do all things; all things, that is, which belong to duty. The great and good Father above, says, "Go *work* in my vineyard;" says this to each one of us, to the feeblest as well as the strongest, to those that have abused and wronged themselves by past self-indulgence. Go work: this is the great injunction of the gospel to every human being. Thus the religion of Christ offers its appeal to the strongest self-respect and the bravest temper. It repeats no nursery tales to beguile a childish fancy into the persuasion that man is impotent. It deals with ponderous realities about his power and obligation. It offers weighty reasons, and asks a weighty consideration, respecting his ability and work. It gives the instruments and the motives, and demands a service. It takes for granted the capacity of every soul to be holy, and abhor iniquity; to forsake the wicked, and live with the righteous; to work out its own salvation, and to do good in the world: and it expects that capacity will not be disowned nor forfeited. It speaks in the stormy notes of a trumpet. Its tone is animating, not depressing; quickening, not stupefying; inspiring, not disheartening. It calls to *action.* It says, Go *work;* and it promises a fitting reward. And thus it is a message of substantial cheerfulness and encouragement, such as we want at the opening of a new year.

Go work *to-day.* I now emphasize another part of the text; namely, *to-day.* That is, whatever ye find *should* be done, this *do immediately.* Christianity no more allows the postponement of a duty than the neglect of it. The Saviour said, on a certain occasion, "That which thou doest, do quickly." And in accordance with this is the spirit of the whole gospel. Do you ask, Why such urgency? The reasons are as obvious as they are many and strong. Go work *to-day*, because the present is the only opportunity of which you are sure. No one can tell what to-morrow may bring forth. We have no pledge of the continuance of life. We have nothing to depend upon but the mercy of that God to whose service we are required to devote ourselves now.

We look around in vain for those whom we saw here a year ago. Could they appear to us this morning, is there any thing, do you think, that they would urge upon us more earnestly than to discharge immediately the duties which God has laid upon us? In another year, there will be those present in this sanctuary who will have to see places made vacant by death, which are now filled by the living. Yes, brethren, it is certain, that, before that period shall arrive, some of us will be in our graves. That we are all liable to death, at any moment, should incite us to perform the duty of each hour as it passes; for no hour can be recalled, and any hour may be our last on earth.

Go work *to-day*, because procrastination does but render the performance of duty at any time more unlikely. The motives to it may never appear so strong to our minds as they do at present. The subject may not again be pressed upon us; and some change in our circumstances may place us out of the hearing of these calls, and out of the power of using the means with which we are now favored. We may be prevailed upon, by some considerations of pleasure or wealth, to abandon the ordinances of worship. Then, too, by delay, we contract the habit of making excuses, our hearts become more insensible, and the world rivets upon us some new shackle.

Go work *to-day*, because, should you have time

enough allotted you in future, and should you be brought to see the error of your ways, repentance will be bitter, and perhaps of little worth. Certainly it will be bitter. No man, who has the heart of a man in him, can look back, in the moments of awakened moral sensibility, upon a life devoted to sin, without indescribable pain. Why shall we now pursue a course that exposes us to this terrible retribution? It may be, too, that our repentance will be, if it come too late, of no great value. What is thought to be reformation at the eleventh hour is much to be suspected, as only the effect of fear, or as a state of mind produced by the prospect of death, without any sincere love of God and duty.

Go work *to-day*, because the whole life ought to be devoted to piety and virtue. If God has a claim upon us in any period of our existence, it is in the present one. We are as strongly bound to be Christian men and women now, as we shall be when old age arrives, and death is near. Then, too, in proportion to the length of our holy service will be the largeness of our recompense. He who begins to-day to live as a Christian should, will, in the ages that are to come, be greatly better off than he that defers entering on such a life to a day far distant. And, furthermore, let us consider how much sorrow we may prevent by an immediate consecration of ourselves to duty; how many our example may influence for good; how many may be awakened by our determination to serve the Lord betimes. Let us consider also how many may be encouraged to go on in wrong courses by our delay; and how their sufferings, as well as ours, may be increased by our neglect and procrastination.

Go work *to-day*, because the invitations of Heaven are so affectionate and so pressing. Every page of the sacred volume, the voice of nature, and the teachings of Divine Providence, all urge us to the immediate performance of duty. Think of the Father, to whom we are indebted for all things; think of Jesus Christ, who poured out his blood for us; think of the rewards of the good and the shame of the bad; think of the eyes in heaven and on the earth which are bent upon us, to see how we act our part; think of our parents, children, friends, whose own happiness is so intimately bound up in us; think of all there is to incite us to instant duty,—and you will not, you cannot, as it seems to me, delay till another year what all know ought to be done in this.

Son, go work in my *vineyard*. Vineyard! what and where is this? Not a spot far off from us; not a field which another may cultivate in our stead. Every one has his allotted sphere of action, every one his place to work in, and it is near him. First, wherever a man's business is, there is his vineyard. But remember what the whole significance of business is. It is to obtain food and raiment and shelter for ourselves and families. But this is not the only or the chief end of business. It is also ordained to build up and discipline the character; and each day's business is working important results in every active person. Upright and benevolent conduct is converting transient impulse into lasting principle; and so of the opposite: dishonest and mean acts are smiting the soul with paralysis; and, when all the outward results of business shall pass away, the inward results will remain. Business life in general is like the caster's moulding sand: by means of it the spirit is taking enduring forms. The dishonest man's gains are transient; but his soul, that was cramped and debased in acquiring those unmerited gains, is permanent, and God only knows when the injury he has inflicted upon himself can be removed. You have seen the green oak's trunk bent, confined, and measured in its crooked posture; and yet it is nothing to straighten again that sturdy wood, compared with rectifying a spirit that has been warped and twisted by acts of dishonesty and falsehood. My friends, beware of distorting the spirit; business upon vicious principles will most assuredly do it; and therefore God has sent his messengers to say to you, Deal justly, love mercy, walk humbly, and live righteously. Take these thoughts with you, and better ones if you can obtain them, and enter upon this year's business with a clear sight and a worthy purpose. Defraud not thy neighbor, harm not thyself; add, not only to thy wealth, but to thy character.

And here we are reminded, secondly, of the vineyard within, to be cultivated. Every one has an intellect; every one has a heart; every one has mental and moral habits, either in the bud, or in the blossom, or already in fruit. These all require looking after; these all demand to be worked for. Some of them may be growing aright; but labor there must be for their protection and guidance and harvesting. Some of them may be growing wrongly; then so much the more will there be the need of vigilance and toil in the way of correction. Well, therefore, in respect to the inner man, may we heed the command, "Son, go work to-day in my vineyard." — The vineyard of thy *thoughts*. Here thou mayst find something unsettled, something dark, something low. Thou mayst be uninformed or misinformed; thou mayst give little attention where thou shouldst bestow the greatest; or thou mayst be prejudiced where thou fanciest thyself impartial and fair. Go, then, and work for thy thoughts; fix to-day a new starting-point for them; detach them from unworthy objects, and give them a direction Godward and heavenward; increase thy acquaintance with the truth; establish the principles of thy judgment;

bring thy calmness into a harmony; set up within the entire realm of thy thoughts a divine and submissive order, which shall be after the pattern of that eternal one, in the circles of which thou dwellest.—The vineyard of thine *affections*. Here, too, thou mayest meet with much to alter as well as to nourish. Thy heart may be cold; or it may be selfish; or it may be impure; or it may dislike what is good, and hanker after evil. Go, then, and work for thy affections; cleanse them from their soils; brush away the rust and the dust that have gathered upon them from vulgar uses or a base inaction; send them forth with a clearer light and a more blessed efficacy; balance them well, so that no one shall play the tyrant over the others; clear up thy jealousies; restrain thy resentments; extend thy sympathies; strengthen the bonds of love that make thee happier as they draw tighter; enlarge thy generosity; banish the selfishness that is an estrangement from God; bring into a beautiful order the dispositions that bind thee to thy kindred, to thy house, to thy friendships, to thy country, and to thy race.—The vineyard of thy *faith*. This, if truly cherished, is a priceless heritage. It stands nobly apart from the world's turmoil, the world's command, and the world's destruction. Thou canst receive no such strength as flows from that. Thou canst receive no such joy as is treasured up in that. Hence must thy truest consolation and courage proceed, when sorrow and depression gather over the heart. But perhaps it has fallen into neglect with thee; perhaps thou hast forgotten its teaching; perhaps thou hast grown insensible to its beauty and to thy soul's deepest want; perhaps thou hast lost the perception of what it is, among thy pleasures and cares; perhaps thou hast allowed a shallow and sluggish scepticism to affront its all-embracing principles. Go, then, and work for thy faith; explore its sources anew; follow again the thread of its evidences; retrace its heavenly law; revive its dying glory; renew the kingdom of the divine and the immortal in the breast that will soon cease to beat. Bring back that old saving faith, though it cost thee much hard work; bring it back, though at the sacrifice of what the passions most crave; bring it back, though in the face of many discouragements; bring it back in its simplicity, in its sovereign beauty, in its reasonableness, and in its might. For he who enters upon a new year without faith is like him who goes to sea in a ship having neither rudder nor anchor.

Brethren and friends, thus represented, does not the Christian life appear practicable and beautiful? There is nothing in it either of mysticism or gloom. It is a plain matter, which commends itself to reason and to conscience. It provides at once for all business pursuits and for all personal culture. The command is, "Go work to-day in my vineyard." In other words, we are bidden to *act*, to act *now*, and to act with Christian purpose in our appropriate field of duty. And if we do this, whatever our task be, whether it relate to outward things or to the inner man, then it is that we do the work of religion. Can we not thus bring religion down to the companionship of our daily life; or rather, I should say, raise our daily life to a companionship with religion? Thus we make religion a practical thing, which it was designed to be, and not a solitary dweller in the cloister, or a divinity sitting coldly in the temple, to which we are to bow the knee in distant homage, but never to take to our hearts and carry with us into the busy world. Thus each year, each month, week, and day, are made Christian. We do not throw on the future a burden of repentance and sorrow. We are not like the son who said, "I go, and went not;" and, when our final day shall come, we shall only have the work of a single day to perform, and not a long account to adjust of past time mis-spent or abused. We shall have but to bow our heads, and go in peace, commending our spirits to the Father.

V.

THE POWER OF EXAMPLE.

1 Tim. iv. 12: "BE THOU AN EXAMPLE OF THE BELIEVERS, IN WORD, IN CONVERSATION, IN CHARITY, IN SPIRIT, IN FAITH, IN PURITY."

EXAMPLE, as everybody allows, at least in words, has great power. In this respect, it stands far above precept. You may give the best advice; but little will it avail, if your own behavior contradicts it. *Words* of wisdom, in order to work much good, must be followed by *deeds* of wisdom. Prescribed rules of conduct are needful; but visible obedience to them is greatly more effective. Ethics taught every community wants; yet it is served far better by ethics practised by the teacher. Moral precept only points out the way we should tread, while example urges us onward in that way. The law-*giver* is not without his use; but the law-*keeper* exerts a vastly larger influence for good. He who *speaks* to us of duty may confer a benefit; but he who, in our sight, *performs* every duty, is our greatest benefactor. What a difference there must have been, in respect to salutary influence, between the precepts of Jesus in the abstract, and Jesus ever acting, — ever showing their practicableness and their blessed efficacy in his life! Vastly more were his disciples formed by his conduct than by his doctrine. They, indeed, received his *teaching* as law; but his *living* was more than law. Law only shows what is right, only prescribes what ought to be done; speaking to the intellect rather than to the heart. But Christ's example illustrated and enforced this law, appealing to the eye, and addressing itself, not only to the understanding, but to the affections; and what the affections are interested in is likely to do most for the character.

Nor, my friends, are any of *us* so conditioned, as not, by our example, to exert a power for evil or for good. Two important truths are involved in this statement, which I beg you to consider. The first of these truths is, that we are all sending out from us an influence which is producing, surely though gradually and imperceptibly, its legitimate effects upon those with whom we associate. This influence depends not, for the time being, upon our own wills. It is constantly going forth, whether we will or not. It depends simply upon what we are; and what we are is the result of what we have been and done. The only way in which our wills and wishes can alter this influence is simply by their effect in altering our characters. It may be our will and our wish to become eminently wise and good; and we may be moved by this purpose and desire to put forth the efforts necessary to secure high attainments in moral and religious excellence. But, when we have done this, the influence which may proceed from us will merely be in harmony with our characters still; will be holy as they are holy, and more or less powerful as they are more or less advanced in holiness. For the second truth is, that the influence which we thus exert by our example will correspond *in its nature* with the peculiarities by which our own characters are distinguished, and will correspond also, *in its power over others*, with the strength, energy, and prominence of these same distinguishing peculiarities. From these two truths it follows, as a practical lesson of great importance, that what we would make others, we must be ourselves; and that in order to do our families, our church, and the community the most good by our example, we must, in our persons, attain to the highest measure of intrinsic moral and religious worth; for I deem futile the outward seemingly good acts of men, whose interior life is corrupt, but whose policy is, Do this or that useful thing for the sake, as they say, of example.

How eminently practical, as well as important, these brief suggestions are, you at once perceive. But do they not, at the same time, possess a heart-moving solemnity? Is it true, that from each of us an influence is constantly going forth to affect others for weal or for woe? and is this influence doing evil or good, according as our *real character* is vicious or virtuous? How, then, can we but be exceedingly anxious about the qualities of the life we are living? Should we any longer be indifferent to the interior principles and feelings and habits we possess; contenting ourselves, as the way of many is, with making our outward actions square with the rules of moral propriety? Oh! let us not be deceived. Just consider: a man may talk about piety and virtue like an angel; may inculcate the truths of religion upon his children with great directness, earnestness, and frequency; and may externally obey all the precepts of the decalogue: while yet, at home, in business, and in society, he may be a low-minded, hard-hearted, mean-spirited, and bad-intentioned wretch. What can *his* example do? The power of his direct verbal inculcation of religious duty, and of his outward observance of moral rules, will be counteracted by the silent influence, which, in his very air and look and manner, he conveys into the hearts of those in contact with him. Again, a man may be a firm supporter of the institutions of the gospel, a constant attendant upon the services of the sanctuary, an earnest advocate of peculiar doctrines, often expressing his approval of the ministrations of the pulpit, ever ready to give from his wealth to the poor; and yet he may breathe around him, from his inmost soul, upon all who associate with him, such a base spirit of worldliness and sensuality as will effectually close all their hearts against whatever he says or does. What can *his* example do, except to grieve the good, and alienate yet more the bad?

And now, my friends, having made these general remarks on the power of example, and its essential connection with character, I must be permitted, in the plainest and most direct manner, to address myself to that class of my hearers for whom this discourse is chiefly intended; namely, all those who, in the relation either of parents or guardians, have the charge of the young. I shall assume that we are already aware of the great responsibility that rests upon us. May I not also suppose that it is our intent to do all in our power to help the children under our care in the formation of a highly moral and religious character? But what is our own example doing to effect this object? We all say, then, — and I take it for granted we are sincere in the assertion, — that our design to secure to our children a good moral and religious education was formed many years ago; and that, ever since, we have professed it to be our desire and endeavor to prosecute this worthy design to its entire accomplishment. So far, we deserve commendation. God bless all such purposes and aims, and crown them with abundant success!

But, my friends, suppose we just pause here a moment, and ask ourselves what influence our own example is exerting, all the while that our wishes and exertions, in other respects, are so praiseworthy?

Do any of us say, we are very careful about what we *do* before our children? Yes; but are we equally careful about what we *are?* We should remember, that, as already more than once said, the influence of example comes less from outward action than from internal character.

Do any of us say, we often *speak* to our children of the importance of piety and good morals? But, my friends, do we show, in our *manner* of speech and in our mode of life, that we ourselves *feel* the importance of what we thus recommend? Words, in this matter, have little effect, when the spirit is wanting.

Do any of us say, we spare no pains to explain and inculcate the precepts of the gospel? But, my friends, do our children see in us proofs of a deep interest in these topics of instruction? Truth of heart and of voice is above all truth of doctrine, and will ensure success more than any other means. Young ears can distinguish the tones of earnest sincerity from those of pretence; and vain, without earnest sincerity, are all a parent's teachings.

Do any of us say, we are always referring our children to the Bible as the best of books? But, my friends, do we read the Bible ourselves?— and with what tokens of reverence and love for its contents? It is not the verbal advice, be assured, but the known tastes of the parent's inmost mind, that form the child's habits.

Do any of us say, we are careful to remind our sons and daughters of the good God, and bid them pray to him night and morning? But, my friends, how do they see us affected by the divine presence? and then do they often find us in the attitude of prayer, and hear our voice in devout supplication? or, if so, can they discern nothing therein but signs of the heart's engagedness in the service? It is but little that a few cold words, from an indifferent soul, can do for a child's piety, whether they be employed in discoursing of God, or whether they be used in prayer to him: the *reality* of a devout spirit within the parent's own bosom is nearly all that is effectual.

Do any of us say, we are at the cost of having seats in the neighboring church, and make it a point that our children shall be constant attendants on public worship? Very well: we could not do less as wise parents. But, my friends, how is it with ourselves in regard to the great privilege and duty of public worship? And if we, from indolence or for the sake of some self-indulgence, stay away from the sanctuary half the time, how can we expect that the younger members of our family will be regularly there? Hardly any thing surprises or pains me more, than the well-known fact, that many fathers, in other respects quite worthy and respectable, are so inconsistent and so thoughtless of the power of example, as to resign themselves to their couch, or to the luxury of a newspaper and cigar, on Sunday afternoon, and let their pew in the church be occupied, if occupied at all, only by the mother and the children. The very look of this, brethren, is bad enough; but the effect of it on the family is far worse.

Do any of us say, we are always in God's house, when it is opened for religious service,— we and our offspring? So far as this is true, it is creditable to us: we could not do a better thing; we thereby perform a duty we owe at once to ourselves, to our families, to the parish of which we are members, to the community at large, and to God. Were we to neglect it, we ought, as it seems to me, to hang our heads in shame. But, my friends, with what dispositions do we go to church? Do we always keep awake there? Do we carry to the sanctuary minds and hearts in harmony with the spirit of the place? Do we show, by our demeanor in the temple of the Most High, that we take an interest in its holy exercises, and that we are truly anxious to derive spiritual nourishment to our own souls? These are pertinent questions; for children are sharp-sighted and apt imitators; and generally they will estimate the value of public worship, not only by our frequency of attendance, but by the signs of interest we ourselves manifest in the services. And here is the place to say, that one of the lamentable tendencies of the present age is to think too much of the sermon, and too little of the devotions. Parents in the morning ask, Who is to *preach* to-day? and in the evening exclaim, We have had a splendid discourse; or, 'Twas but a miserable homily. Not a word do they say, not a thought do they seem to entertain, about holding communion with God, which, after all, is the chief purpose of assembling on the Lord's day. And as with the parents, so with the children. They catch the same spirit; and, instead of going regularly to their accustomed place of meeting to *worship* in sincerity and in truth, they soon learn to stay at home; or they become rovers, hunting for the hall or church where some *star preacher* is to hold forth, especially if he has been advertised in the newspapers as one who is to speak on some *interesting* or novel subject.

Do any of us say, we see to it that our children attend regularly the Sunday school? So far, so good. But with what sentiments do we regard this institution? How much do we know of it? Is it often that we inquire about it? Do we frequently visit it? or when our little son or daughter returns from it with a full heart, glowing countenance, and impatient tongue, and begins to tell us of some instructive and affecting exercise which took place there, — which most engages our attention, the account which the child gives, or the frivolous book that happens to be in our hand? Ah, my erring brethren! happy for our offspring that there are such institutions as Sunday schools! but we are preventing half their blessed effects by our manifest preference for something of less importance.

Do any of us say, that we are continually cautioning our children against too strong an attachment to the passing objects of time and sense; that we tell them to set their supreme affections on things above; that we teach them that virtue and piety are vastly superior to the artificial distinctions of wealth, fashion, office, pleasure, and outward display; and that we always advise them to respect and love most, and to select for their associates and friends, those who stand highest in point of moral and religious excellence? Well, in all this we do right. But, my friends, how do we practise in regard to these particulars? The objects of time and sense, — how is it with them? What do our children see to be uppermost in our minds, — truth and virtue and heaven, or money and every earthly thing by which our vanity can be gratified, and our appetites sated? What is the great, absorbing topic of conversation in our families, from morning to evening? Is it, wherewithal we shall enlighten the mind, improve the heart, ennoble and adorn the character, that so we may open within ourselves never-failing sources of true dignity and happiness? or is it, wherewithal we shall eat and drink, and add to our treasures, and furnish our houses in richer style, and outdo our neighbors in dress and equipage, and move conspicuously in the highest walks of society? And in respect to the good counsels given to children, as to whom they should most respect and choose for their associates, what strange delusion many parents seem to be under in this regard! Why, my friends, to-morrow, some personage, very rich, high in office, and accustomed to shine in what the gay world calls the first circles, but one of very questionable morals, of small intelligence except as a judge of etiquette and wines, and of no pretensions to religious faith or feeling, is to dine with us, let me suppose. Well, it is considered by us as a great event, and it will be talked of as such in our family till the hour of the appointment arrives. And then the toil of preparation, then the deferential greetings, then the profoundly respectful attentions; then the emphatic assurances of sincerest regard, and so forth. Now, our children have eyes and ears; they have minds, too, and can draw an inference. But take the counterpart to the scene. Next day, an individual of another sort is to visit us. His intellect, his heart, his morals, his religion, his whole character, are such as do honor to human nature. Than he, there is not in the city a man intrinsically better. We know him to be a sincere worshipper of God, a generous lover of mankind, a true disciple of Christ. But he happens not to rank among the wealthy; he lives in a small house, holds no conspicuous office, makes little show, and is seldom seen in what is *called* fashionable, but which often really *is* vulgar society. This good man enters our dwelling at the hour appointed. The inmates had scarcely bestowed a thought on his coming. All seems very much in the family as if no one were with them but their own members. Though entertaining one of the purest and noblest of men, they give no signs of special effort; indeed, one might say, they are hardly respectful; for their guest is not the world's talk, but only *a* worthy man. Now, as I said before, children have eyes and ears; and they have a certain faculty, also, by which from simple premises they can reason out a conclusion. What, then, let me ask, avails all a parent's *verbal teaching* about the importance of preferring moral to worldly distinctions, while he thus allows his children to see his example giving the lie to his precepts? If we, fathers and mothers, do, in daily practice, honor those who are distinguished only because they chance to be rich, and in office, and in the first class of showy society, while, at the same time, we slight, for their poverty and obscure position, the really intelligent, the truly moral, and the sincerely religious, why, then, we must not marvel if our children grow up with the like preferences; if they, too, choose for their companions the outwardly prosperous rather than the inwardly virtuous, and strive more for the artificial distinctions of this fleeting world than for the genuine excellences which alone God approves, which alone gain the respect of truly wise and good men, and which alone can qualify one for the happiness of heaven.

But I need not pursue the subject further. You have received, from the instances already cited, the leading idea it was chiefly my desire to convey: it is, that, in morals and religion, *example* does the most essential part of education. This, by itself, when correct, will work wonders. Without it, all else will be ineffectual. The one great impression I am mainly anxious to have every parent bear away with him is, that he who would make his children truly good must be good himself. We cannot explain subjects with much practical effect, on which we have not ourselves thought; we cannot give efficacy to truths which we do not ourselves feel; we cannot inspire hopes by which our own minds are not animated;

and it will be in vain for us to inculcate motives from which we do not act. In other language, we are educating our children, not so much by particular lessons, indispensable as these are, as by our daily conversation; by the feelings and sentiments which we habitually express; by the motives from which we act, or appear to act; or, in fine, by the whole power of our example, the whole influence of our character. "Be ye, then, *examples* of the believers, in word, in conversation, in charity, in spirit, in faith, in purity." And God grant us the blessedness of seeing our dear children growing up in the virtues and graces of the holy gospel!

VI.

COUNSELS FOR YOUNG MEN.

Titus ii. 6: "Young men likewise exhort."

In attempting, this morning, to obey the injunction of the apostle in the text, by means of a few words of advice addressed to that interesting portion of my audience who have now reached the period of life when they are taking, or are about to take, their first steps in the highway of the world, by themselves and for themselves, I feel myself embarrassed by the multiplicity of topics which crowd upon attention, connected with the very brief space of time to which my remarks must be restricted. But no matter for this, comparatively, if—the good-will of my hearers concurring—I can, in any way, throw out a few hints, dictated by sincere regard, that shall be of use to the young men here present.

You have now, my friends, arrived at the most important period of your life. This is true as regards yourselves. You are about to assume responsible stations; to act from your own judgment, and upon your own principles; to sow what you shall, by and by, reap; to take your destinies, as it were, into your own hands. Can any thought be more serious? any, more affecting? The same is true, also, as respects others. You are soon to succeed your fathers in the high pursuits of society. Its burdens you must bear; its interests will be committed to you. The aspects of the present will take much of its coloring from you; and around you the hopes of the future cluster. Aged patriotism, philanthropy, and piety turn their dim eyes to you, and behold, as in a mirror, the promise of coming years. *Your* hands will soon be upon the golden cords of society, which are its bonds of conservation; and, in a little while, it will depend upon you, whether they shall be weakened or made stronger, whether they shall be preserved or torn asunder. Can such considerations fail to awaken in you the serious and earnest inquiry, "How can we acquit ourselves worthily?"

In answer to a question of this kind, which it is becoming in every young person to ask, permit me to remark in the outset, and with emphasis, that there is one way, and only one way, in which you can either fulfil aright your obligations to society, or secure truly your own welfare; and that is, by means of a thoroughly good character. This no one will deny, and therefore I need not stop to prove it. But I *may* be told that those I am speaking to have come forth from their homes and schools with characters already well formed, already educated for every duty of life. Now, no one will concede more on this score than myself. Ready and happy I am to grant that the class of young men whom I address are behind no others of their age and opportunities, in regard to the good intellectual and moral habits they have acquired. But *this* question, nevertheless, I must be allowed to ask, — Is their education now to stop? Is their character to-day all that it is expected or desired to be hereafter? Whatever others may suppose, do not you, my young friends, indulge any such idea for a moment. By no means deem your education finished. Presume not to measure your future intellectual, moral, and religious character by the standard at which you have now arrived, high as this may be. Bear it in mind, all along, that both your own highest good and the well-being of the community depend on your making yet further and ever perpetual progress. Dream not that God put you on this earth merely to get a living; and that, when you have been educated sufficiently for this, you have done all, in the way of preparation, that your true interests and those of society require. No: take higher, wider, and further-reaching views. See and feel that the great object you should have always before you is a progressive education, a continually improving character. This is my first counsel; and there can be none of greater moment. Let me now proceed to say a few words, as to what must be done, on your part, in order to secure the constant advancement to which I have referred, and so to be enabled to fulfil, for yourselves and for the world, the ends for which you are created.

1. In the first place, enter upon the active scenes of life before you with worthy aims. From the very outset, be it your desire and purpose to act for the *true* ends of human existence. Never indulge the thought, for an instant, that your only or your chief concern should be to amass vast wealth. Remember that you have a mind, which is of infinitely greater value than all outward things; and see to it that the due cultivation of your faculties be the object of your highest ambition. Do nothing, submit to nothing, that will tend to lessen or obscure in your sight this great end of your being. In all the toils and all the trials of your earthly career, never forget this most important of human concerns. Fix your eye, from the beginning, upon this shining mark; and let the strongest forces of your nature be brought to bear in the path that leads directly to it. Consider, often, why you are here, what you are, whither you are journeying, what is your chief duty, and what should be your prime object. Take this thought with you into all the

scenes of the world. Resolve to act faithfully upon it, from this day forward. Cling to it in prosperity and adversity, amid the cheerful sunshine and calm of life, and when you are tempest-tost under dark clouds and on rough seas. Thus regard early and ever the true ends of existence, and you will have one of the best securities for happiness and for improvement of character.

2. In the next place, have an eye to circumstances, and seek such as will be favorable to your growth in excellence. Character being the main thing, why, for any consideration of wealth or station, will a young man put himself where its purity and progress will be sacrificed? And yet how many overlook this in their choice of a pursuit or of a place of residence! For the sake of making money a little faster, they will go where there are no books, no churches, no improving society. I caution you against this transgression of an obvious law of wisdom. I counsel you to consider well, when deliberating on the kind of business you shall engage in or the spot where you shall dwell, what will be likely to be the sort of circumstances connected therewith, that will affect your intellectual, moral, and religious character. This advice, surely, you will not, if you reflect a moment, regard as any other than the dictate of the soundest good sense. For why should one, made in the image of God and destined to immortality, hazard the chief end of

his being? — why put in jeopardy his principal interests, by selecting, without reference to them, his place, his occupations, or his companions; and, through this carelessness, be all his life long, perhaps, striving against the stream, struggling under the deleterious influence of an unhealthy moral atmosphere?

3. But, in the third place, it is not enough to start in life with a high aim, and under favorable circumstances. These alone never made a perfect man. Would you be what you may and ought? You must, then, be active, — active, I mean, not only about your ordinary business, but, so far as you can, in whatever appertains to the true interests of a human being. Character — which I am all along regarding as the chief concern — is not only *expressed* by actions: it is formed, and made to grow, by them. True, its foundation is laid in thought, disposition, purpose; but it is built up and established by action. Sentiments of virtue die out from the soul, unless they gain substance and life by corresponding deeds. Hence the lamentable fact, that so many of those who come forth glowing with youthful ardor for whatever is praiseworthy soon find their generous sensibilities deadened; and they become selfish and sordid, and, in the same proportion, stationary or retrograde in character. No better advice can be given, therefore, to young men, for their own welfare, — to say nothing of

society's need of their services,—than that, as soon as they enter upon responsible life, they look carefully around them, and inquire, where and how they can act, in behalf of the intellectual, moral, and religious enterprises of the times. Let no one, I beseech him, if he means to be any thing worthy of his nature and opportunities,—let no one content himself with the mere routine of his common business: not that I would have him neglect this; but let him so arrange his affairs, that he may have frequent intervals of leisure, however short, wherein he can express in action the high sentiments he has learned to cherish for the great moral interests of the community. Let him, from the first, be among those who stand forth, with true hearts and ready hands, to oppose the current of vice; to uphold the integrity and honor of principle; to determine the suffrage of right; to maintain truth, morality, and religion in their supremacy; and to help forward every worthy and useful end for the good of society and the country. And let all young men know and feel, that, just in proportion to their fidelity in acting out pure and generous sentiments for the common advantage, they minister to their own strength and elevation of principle, and advance their own character towards perfection.

4. But, my young friends, I must be allowed to commend to you yet another step. All that I

have pointed out you may do, and still your character may fall short of the true standard. Add, then, let me say, in the fourth place,—add to what has already been suggested, strict moral and religious *self-discipline.* Character can stand on nothing that is outward. It must be built up from within. The complete man, the perfect human being, is, can be, made such only upon principle. In respect to nothing have you reason to feel greater solicitude than for this; not for a season only, but all along your future career. Self-discipline,—moral and religious self-discipline,—here is the true though secret cause of every really noble character that the world has produced. Neglect not, I beseech you,—neglect not a means of such efficacy, and without which all others may avail little. Often retire from the turmoil of business and the resorts of pleasure, to commune with your own heart. Study the principles from which you act, and see if they are all right. Ascertain in what respects you have erred, that so you may know where to apply the correcting hand. Hold converse with the pure and good, and thus avail yourselves of the benefit of sympathy and counsel. That you will read books, hear lectures, and be constant attendants at church, I of course take for granted; but this, by itself, will never suffice: you must see to it, that you always go to these exercises with active minds, disposed and prepared by self-discipline to derive the advantage they are fitted, only on that condition, to impart. Especially, and above all, it is necessary that the spirit of a pure and earnest religion bear sway among your faculties. Early, therefore, consecrate your hearts to God, and ever make him the most constant object of regard. Ally yourselves to him, to his counsels and his purposes, and secure the co-operation of his will. In the deep life of the spirit, commune with him, and thus nourish yourselves in all goodness. In the affectionate imitation of Jesus Christ, commend yourselves to his blessing, and so find strength and peace. In the hope and prospect of a happy futurity, toil on, rejoicing and persevering through good report and evil report; knowing that your witness is in heaven, and your record on high. But I must check myself. Of the importance of character, and of the way in which it is to be advanced, no more can be said at present. Yet a few words you will allow me to add, as suggestive of motives, respecting your position, responsibleness, and influence.

My friends, are you fully aware of these motives? They are such as give you a power for good, which no language can adequately describe; and, if your character shall be all I have been asking for, what blessings may not present and future generations receive through you!

Consider the peculiar station you occupy. You

stand next to the acting and influential ones now upon the stage of busy life; and many of you are treading in the footsteps and supplying the places of those who are passing from it. Upon you begins to rest already the ark of our freedom; in you dwell the powers that must decide the character of the coming age. To go no further than this city, what interests are soon to come into your hands, — the government, the schools, the churches, all our cherished institutions! How do you purpose to use these vast instrumentalities of good? Worthily? "Yes!" you are all, I doubt not, ready to exclaim. God grant that you may! But remember, I beseech you, your peculiar position, and the responsibilities connected with it.

Consider next the times you live in. Never, in the annals of the world, was there a period so interesting, in many respects, as this. I need not, or, were it otherwise, the passing hour would not permit me to describe it. But I wish you to study the aspect of the age, the aspect of affairs, and then act wisely and diligently in reference to it. It is for you to lay hold upon the great principles for good awakened in these latter days by Christianity, and urge them forward. In order to discharge your obligations aright, you must examine the signs of the times; must know how to preserve what is good, and to correct what is bad, in prevailing sentiments and principles. You must be alive and vigilant and active; feeling, at every step, how much will depend upon your character and efforts.

Consider, again, what facilities and opportunities you have for benefiting yourselves and the community. The means of education are extending, and its standard rising. The press is active as it never was before, and science is revealing new wonders every day. The instrumentalities for conveying intelligence and persons throughout the land are increasing with astonishing rapidity. Then, too, our republican principles and institutions, — what could be better than these for the prospects of young men? Again, the priceless light of the gospel, with all its privileges and all its blessings, is beaming full around you. And now let me ask, Have you any excuse, if you do not work, as others have never done, for yourselves and for mankind? Will you not faithfully perform the duties which such means and opportunities imply? May not our schools, our churches, our municipal affairs, our general politics, all the interests of learning, of philanthropy, of freedom, and religion, look to you for that sort of character and effort which will cause them to be not only preserved, but improved, for the coming generations?

Consider, yet further, the place where you live, and the immense territory over which the principles and sentiments, as well as the merchandise, that are to go out hence, must spread. What a centre is not this metropolis destined, under the smiles of Divine Providence, to become, — what a centre, whence wholesome influences may be diffused far and wide! How important that these influences be of the best sort! If this city of ours is to be one of the great radiating points of intelligence to the whole land, as it has been and is to New England, it is of the utmost importance that it should be eminently the seat of all moral and religious excellences. The light of the body politic is the eye; and, if that eye be healthy, the whole body shall be full of light. And for this we must look mainly to our young men. Will they prove themselves adequate to the exigency? I call on them to understand their responsible position, and to conduct themselves in it worthily. I adjure them not to be wholly absorbed by the zeal of commercial enterprise, which so kindles and pushes forward this great and growing community; but to devote themselves, in due measure, to those far higher interests of intellect, morals, and religion, in respect to which such multitudes, all over the land, will look here for a pattern and a motive. Just glance to the North, to the South, and to the far West bounded by the Pacific, and consider that into all those regions your goods will go; and, what is of vastly greater moment, that in all those regions your principles and characters will be known. Reflect, too, in this relation, on what the country is growing to be. Is it to have a population of fifty millions, before many of us, now living, shall die? Is this population to swell, within the compass of a century, to two hundred millions? and, in less than two centuries, is it to equal half the present population of the globe? And is the character of this mighty mass of human beings to be fixed, in no small degree, by those who are now living and acting? And can you count it of little consequence what sentiments you imbibe, what habits you form, and what influences you throw around you? Nor is this all. Think, moreover, of the amazing resources of your country, and of the influence she must exert in coming centuries over the destinies of the world. And reflect that *you* are now giving character to that mighty influence. For one, I tremble in view of the responsibilities which rest upon the young men of this land, and especially upon those who live in large cities, out of which must go a controlling power. God has attached to their existence an importance incomparably surpassing that of any equal portion of the human family. He is giving them the means pre-eminently to bless the world. And the alternative, also, of cursing it, is one, from the result and consequences of which, if they choose it, they cannot escape. Oh! if you will enter upon a manhood of mere fashion, of vice, of worldliness, of low ambition; if you will pass through life without God, and die without virtue,—better that your abode were in some obscure island of the sea, or some region of the north, locked in eternal winter, or some desert scorched by a vertical sun, than in this garden of creation!

But I would hope, I *will* hope, better things. I will hope that you may imbibe and cherish a right spirit, and allow yourselves to be habitually swayed by pure, elevated, and noble principles. I will hope that you may form worthy characters; that you may possess and exhibit the grand features of Christian piety and virtue in such pre-eminence as to impress them deeply on those around, and those who shall come after you. I will hope that you may aspire to the dignity of leading lives, while on earth, that all the wise and good will delight to refer to as examples; and of leaving, when you ascend to heaven, an influence which shall give light and purity and salvation to future millions. No age, no spot in creation, has presented to it greater advantages for Christian effort and success; and the youth of mind or of wealth who shall catch the spirit of a Howard or a Washington may now fix an image upon the world as fair and indelible as theirs.

VII.

COUNSELS FOR YOUNG WOMEN.

Titus ii. 4: "ALSO, TEACH THE YOUNG WOMEN."

IT must be obvious, my hearers, to reflecting persons, that a preacher may add to his usefulness, by occasionally addressing his instructions to particular classes of persons; and this, as you are aware, has not unfrequently been my practice. While most of my sermons have been designed for those who are in mature and active life, irrespectively of their age, their sex, or their peculiar relations and duties, I have, once and again, spoken especially to children, also to parents, then to the aged, and likewise to the youth of the congregation generally, without regard to the difference of male and female. This last distinction, however, I ventured to observe, Sunday before last, as some of you may remember, in a discourse devoted entirely to what seemed to me the interests of *young men;* and the same thing I propose to do on the present occasion, inviting the other sex of a like age, who are accustomed to worship here, to receive from me some hints, kindly suggested, respecting the duties that devolve upon them. Nor can I, perhaps, begin with any remark deserving greater heed than this one, important certainly as it is trite; namely, that, if there be a single part of life more momentous than another, it is doubtless the season of youth; the time, I mean, when the dependence of childhood is over, and the burdens of mature years have not yet been assumed. It is a period when the mind is called, if ever, to put itself into a posture for serious meditation; when it should look about it, and send its thoughts forward, and settle for itself some determinate rules of conduct. Up to this point, my young friends, you have been led by the wisdom and affection of others: from this point you will, most of you, have to decide for yourselves the great questions of duty. The period has arrived, or is fast approaching, when, in all essential respects, you must assume, as free agents, an undivided responsibility for the feelings you cherish, the deeds you perform, the principles you adopt, and the influence you exert. Of course, it is a time that should seem to you one of great interest; from a right use of it will flow consequences of the utmost value; and it is sadly misapplied by those who give it all up to thoughtless gayety.

And now, what is the counsel of *wisdom* to

you in this most important period of your life? Her voice addresses you in mild but earnest tones, telling you that every thing depends on right principles and a good character. Wisdom points to the relations you now sustain, and the duties they involve, and says that in these you cannot be either useful or happy, without pure sentiments and virtuous habits. She bids you look forward to the *new* stations you must fill, and to know and feel betimes how ample should be your preparation of mind and heart for the proper discharge of the obligations which will devolve upon you there. Presuming that you are not indisposed to listen, for a little while at least, to some such counsels of practical wisdom as these, I crave the privilege of proceeding to say a few words in accordance with her wholesome suggestions respecting your present and future spheres of duty; hoping thereby to furnish some hints that may not be altogether without advantage to that interesting class of my hearers whom it affords me so much pleasure particularly to address.

1. I observe then, first, that, in the common course of things, the duties given to a young woman to perform are the blessed ones of a *good daughter*. A good daughter! There are, indeed, other ministries more conspicuous than hers; but none in which a better spirit is required, and none to which the heart's warm requitals are

more joyfully made. A good daughter! What a treasure is not she to her father! She is the cheering light of his dwelling. The idea of her is indissolubly connected with that of his happy home. The grace and vivacity and purity and tenderness of her sex have their place among the influences that elevate, while they gladden, his spirit. What a charm for him in the melody of her voice! and is there any gloom that yields not to the brightness of her smile? Is there another outward possession that he would not consent to part with sooner than with her? Still more dear, if possible, is a good daughter to a mother's heart. To her, what a ready sharer of domestic cares! what an effective lightener of household burdens! what an ever-present joy and triumph to maternal affection! Indeed, is there any price that could buy of her such a blessing? To both parents, a daughter really deserving the epithet, *good*, is a treasure unutterably precious. She is the delight of their eyes; the object on which their thoughts oftenest centre and blend; the pride and ornament of their hospitality; the gentle nurse of their sicknesses; the constant agent in those unnumbered acts of kindness, which they chiefly care to have rendered because unpretending but all-expressive proofs of love. Oh, how little those daughters know of the power which God has given them, who do not, every time that a parent's countenance turns to them, awaken feelings of rapture in a parent's heart! Whether such be the privilege and joy of *your* father and mother, my young friends, depends upon you, — depends upon your temper and conduct. For their sakes, if for no other reason, be anxious, I beseech you, to cultivate the sentiments, and form the habits, of virtue and piety. If you have any ambition, let it be to requite those to whom you owe so much, and whose happiness depends so greatly on you, by all the genuine exhibitions of a true filial love and devotion.

2. I remark, next, that to a young woman ordinarily belong the duties of a good sister; and how much do not these imply! In the daily intimacies of a well-regulated household, what a blessing is a good sister's influence! Who can measure it? How much is constantly within such a one's power, of whatever helps to make home a pleasant and improving place to those who are objects, with her, of the same parental care! Has she younger sisters? With what a sense of security is confidence reposed in her, and with what assurance that it will be honestly and considerately given is her counsel sought! Of the happiness which they enjoy, of the docility which they manifest, of the improvement which they make, how much depends upon her affectionate and faithful assiduities! Has she brothers? What dependence is not theirs on

her for sympathy, encouragement, and warning! Many are the young men, to whom, when thrown into circumstances of temptation, the thought of a sister's purity and love has been as a constant, holy presence, deterring from every vicious act. None but they who have experienced it can tell how large and cherished a place such a guardian angel's affection can hold in grateful memory, with which a brother, who has been blessed with the benefits of this relation, looks back to the time of his childhood. Let not any of my young hearers who are sisters dream that they can be acting with a light responsibility. A serious charge has been given them, and serious consideration becomes them as to how they fulfil the trust. Never forget, that, in the relation you sustain, you may contribute much, not only to the immediate gratification of those you most dearly love, but also to their improvement and their future happiness. If for no other reason, at least for the sake of brothers and sisters, be good; and let them be won, by your example, to gentleness and truth and piety, to all those excellences which ennoble and adorn the character.

3. I pass now to the duties of young women in society, and let my first words be those of an indulgent allowance. Think not, my friends, that, because my station is in the pulpit, I am going to proscribe the innocent enjoyments of

social intercourse, or to say aught against those reasonable modes of rendering yourselves interesting which persons of your age and sex are so naturally inclined to adopt. But surely I may remind you,—and it affords me satisfaction to believe you will concur in the propriety of the remark,—that no young woman who goes into society merely to gratify a love of pleasure, or, what is worse, merely to indulge feelings of vanity in the display of superior personal attractions, is acting either wisely or dutifully. Self-improvement and a regard to others' good are higher motives, and by these you ought to be influenced. If your elders are bound to be rational and considerate and useful, so are you, at least to a certain extent. If they are able to go into society with the purpose and power to purify and elevate, while they grace it, so, in your measure, are you able; and, believe me, this your measure is not small. For the very attractions which naturally belong to young women, and the sense of which, if you are light-minded and vain, may bewilder and lead you into hurtful follies, give you, when discreet and sensible, a vast power to improve the tastes and sentiments and characters of the other sex. Here is a trust of serious magnitude. The moral influence which, by means of the peculiar interest it excites, the female mind, duly cultivated and rightly employed, may exert in a community over those especially whose sentiments and habits are forming, is altogether beyond estimation. Be aware, I beseech you, of this; and see to it, that the bearing of your whole conduct, in every social circle, be decidedly on the side of what is pure and true and correct. Never utter a deceptive word, nor do a wrong deed, for the sake of another's favor, though thereby you might gain a fortune or a throne. Do not, on any consideration, countenance and encourage either the conduct or the language of those whose company you keep, when that conduct or that language seems to you to border, in the least, on what is immoral. Smile approvingly on no attempts at wit or humor, by which modesty can be made to blush, or the humblest character, whether present or absent, is caused to appear in a false and unfavorable light. Frown on all insincere protestations, on all flatteries addressed to yourselves, and on all malignant surmises or slanders uttered against others. Let pertness and foppery, and the whole tribe of kindred follies, so intrusive and annoying in some circles of young people at the present day, be driven, by your prompt and marked disapprobation, into the obscurity from which they should never have presumed to emerge. Allow neither irreligious scepticism nor canting hypocrisy, neither coarse sentiments under the guise of polished manners, nor treacherous principles veiled in the language of honorable professions, nor vicious propensities associated with the show of wealth and fashion, be thought by any one to gain from you either a look or a word that does not imply a rebuke; while you will permit, always and everywhere, pure tastes, right feelings, noble thoughts, and all that appertains to elevated morals and to a simple and earnest piety, to flourish under the smiles of your favor, like the flowers under the blessed sunshine of spring.

So much, my friends, in respect to the duties of young women, as daughters, sisters, and members of society. Even for these duties, to say nothing of others, whether at present incumbent or hereafter to devolve on them, what trait of a truly good character is not needful? Can you name a single habit of mind, of heart, or of conduct, sanctioned and required by virtue and religion, that will not find scope in these relations? Were you, then, always to remain as young as you now are, and never to enter other and wider spheres of exertion and influence, ample reason there would be for all possible efforts on your part to possess and exhibit every quality of character which the wise and good regard and recommend as thoroughly excellent.

What, then, must not be your sense of responsibleness, and what your eager desire and strenuous endeavor to improve yourselves more and more, when you consider, that, with added years, you will incur new obligations; that soon you will find yourselves in other stations, where no measure of intelligence, no strength of principle, no virtue, no piety, will be more than adequate to secure your own highest welfare, or to further the best interests of the community! These new obligations, these other stations, I need not specify. To know them, you need only to look among your elders. Such a survey will show you how various and how far extended should be a woman's acquirements. You will find, I think, that more is requisite on her part than many who have given no thought to the subject suppose. True, women are not to be qualified to be sailors or soldiers or lawyers or statesmen; they are not to be trained for the toil of the camp, the bar, the senate chamber, or the pulpit; yet, certainly, God and nature destined them to spheres that demand very various and extensive culture. As to general knowledge, it should, at least, be such as shall acquaint them with the nature and uses both of the body and the mind; the scope and force of all their powers, alike physical, intellectual, and moral; the essential laws of the creation around them; general history and Christianity; and the best works of morality, religion, sentiment, and taste. Their aim, from first to last, most surely should be to improve all their faculties as much as possible; to ascertain clearly the way of their duty, and to be enabled to walk in it in the most acceptable, faithful, and becoming manner; to enlarge their usefulness to the utmost extent of their ability; to give a virtuous direction to all the influences which God has imparted to them; to fill up their leisure time with what is not only pleasurable, but profitable; to dignify and adorn the station in which they are placed; to provide themselves with elevated principles and sure consolations, such as shall sustain them in adversity and in the hour of death, and to enable them so to live on earth, that they may live happily in heaven.

So much, at least, it should be the wish and the endeavor of every young woman to attain. Such cannot but be her wish and endeavor, if she has been a careful observer of what her elders have found indispensable to their highest success, and if, at the same time, she is true to her nature, her destination, her fellow-beings, and her God. And now, my young friends, will you not be disposed to take good heed that none of us, who are in advance of you in years, shall have occasion to fear for you? When so much depends on your own exertions, as regards both the present and future, will you not see to it, that your thoughts take a right direction, your feelings become interested in whatever is true and useful, and your efforts be engaged in all that ministers to self-improvement, and promises benefit to society? Can you, when so much is at stake, pass these your golden days in indolence or frivolous amusements? Shall your precious hours be given to the follies and vanities of artificial life? Will you allow heartless fashion or no less heartless literature to corrupt the best feelings and destroy the noblest energies of your soul? Let your good sense, your conscience, your pride, either or all of these answer, and sure I am the decision will be right. But will every one *abide* by it, amidst the temptations of the world? Alas! what do experience and observation teach? Good sense, conscience, pride, may, for they every day do, prompt right decisions; but how often they fail to carry persons on, without halting or turning aside through the whole length of the way of duty! What is requisite beside? My young friends, I pray you withdraw not attention from me, when I say, in reply, it is *religion.* Believe me, this is the one thing needful. Without this, a young woman, whatever else she may have, is not well furnished for any one of the duties, nor any one of the stations, which I have named, or to which I have alluded. Take from her soul the element of a pure, living piety, and at once my idea of her as a *good* daughter, of a *good* sister, of a *good* occupier of any of the spheres assigned to her in life, becomes incomplete. Chief, therefore, among the counsels I would give to every young woman, is, that she fix early and deeply in her heart the sentiments and principles of a rational and earnest piety. Truly, in urging this topic upon the female sex, I ought to have, on your part, a peculiar readiness of sympathy; and this for many reasons.

In speaking of religion, I of course mean Christianity; and what has not this blessed dispensation done for women? Think of Jesus himself, whom we commemorate to-day,—think of him in relation to women. At the very beginning of his ministry, he showed himself interested in their welfare; and to the hour of his death he continued that work of redemption to which they owe their present elevated state in society. His efforts on their behalf the women of Judea at once appreciated. His earliest friend was a woman; his only steadfast friends through his ministry were women; the last at the cross, and the first at the sepulchre, was a woman. Here, my female auditors, is an example for you. Think what it was, at that perilous period, to avow confidence in Jesus. And will you, in these easy times, be ashamed of Christ? Trace now the workings of the gospel from that age to the present, and see how much you are indebted to it. This it is that has raised your sex from degradation and servitude, and placed you by the side of man, his equal and friend. This it is which has opened to woman treasures of happiness, from which, in all ages and climes, she had been debarred on earth, and joys celestial to which she had never dared to lift an eye of hope. Can you think of this, and not open your mind and heart, even now in your youthful years, to its blessed influences? Consider, moreover, how your distinctive characteristics, how the quick sensibilities, the strong affections, the pure sympathies, of your nature, peculiarly fit you for this religion. It offers to your tender regards a Being infinitely worthy of your love; to your sense of dependence, an Almighty Protector; to your confidence, an unchangeable Friend. It promises to satisfy your every pure and generous aspiration; it delights, if I may so speak, to conduct just such a nature as yours towards perfection. Again, excluded as you must be from the more active and engrossing pursuits of the world, and obliged to be much by yourself, or accompanied only by the members of your household, what opportunities and facilities will you not have for cultivating and cherishing the spirit which Christianity breathes! And besides, where, except in this religion, can you, during many of the lonely hours that must fall to your lot, find the means of satisfying the cravings of your intellect and heart, unless in those truths which Jesus Christ has revealed to the hungering and thirsting soul, — truths that quicken, while they chasten, the fancy; which regulate the enthusiasm they have kindled, and guide the energies they have called forth; truths that offer to woman a relief from the evils incident to solitude, and a solace in the midst of her peculiar trials, — the truths of a spiritual religion. Still further, an argument to the same effect may be drawn from the consideration, that if through female encouragement and example the spirit of the age is to be purified of its folly, if it is to be elevated and adorned by Christian excellence, women must be sincerely and practically religious. Their regard for the gospel must be neither insincere nor superficial; their reverence and love for it must be seated deeply in the heart, and appear conspicuously in the daily life. Let it be known that they are the advocates of a piety which they cherish in their souls, and that they are opposed in principle and habit to every practice inconsistent with the morality of the gospel, and, however great a change *should* be made in the sentiments or usages of the other sex, it *will* be made. For, when the alternative is amendment or exclusion from their favor, hesitation will not long precede choice.

One other thought, my young friends, you must allow me to suggest, though to persons of your age it may seem a gloomy one. It is, that healthy, joyous, and hopeful as you may now be, there are before you in life, as there have been in the path of your elders, trials and sorrows, which you will need the aid of religion to enable you to bear. Surely, you must have learned enough to know that you cannot reasonably expect to be exempt from the changes that fall to the lot of all; let your morning sun shine as radiantly as it will, it must often be darkened; hearts will be divided, and hopes will be destroyed. There are sorrows which follow human passion; there are misfortunes sent by the act of God: you will sit by the side of the sick; you will mourn over the remains of the dead; you will find yourselves, at length, on the brink of your own grave. Whither shall you turn for support and encouragement? Religion, religion, must be your refuge then. There is no other adequate prop and solace in the last hour. Think not that I say this merely in the way of my profession. I would speak to you as a familiar friend, and the truth of my remarks is attested by the dying words of thousands in every Christian age. Be it, then, your care to take with you into life the principles of religion. Do not proceed another step in your journey on earth, without the possession of that which our Saviour told Martha was the one thing needful, and which has been proved to be so by the experience of your sex, in every age, since he left the world.

By the experience of her, let me add, whose lamented death occasioned the special prayer offered this morning for bereaved ones here present. That excellent woman, the faithful wife and devoted mother, as well as good daughter, was, not many years ago, among the young women of this society, one of the most interesting and happy; seeming to have, as much as any other, the promise of a long life. But a fatal disease arrested her in an adjoining city; and, recently, weeping parents and children, brothers and sisters, followed her remains to the grave. What sustained her in her lingering illness? Religion. What reconciled her to the event of death which for months she saw steadily approaching? Religion. What enabled her to find such support and solace in prayer? Religion. What made her feel, when her own strength became weakness and no human arm was adequate to her needs, that there was One, even the Father of her spirit, in whose powerful presence and gracious love she could confide? Religion. What, at the closing scene, caused heaven to open so brightly to her mind, that willingly she could resign whatever, and it was much, that had made her happy on earth, and joyfully pass on, at the call of her God, to meet the blessed realities of the spiritual world? Religion. And, my young friends, be not incredulous when I say that what supported and cheered her in sickness and death, you will want, sooner or later, to support and cheer you. God, of his infinite mercy, grant that no one to whom I now speak may find herself destitute of religion at that time of most urgent need, whenever it shall

12

come! Will this prayer be answered? It depends greatly on yourselves. As you sow, you will reap. No one can reasonably look for a peaceful and happy close of life, who has not begun early to cultivate the principles of virtue and piety; while all who have these in vigorous growth may feel sure of blessedness at last.

VIII.

COUNSELS FOR MOTHERS.

1 Tim. v. 2: "Entreat the elder women as mothers."

It seems to me well, at times, to address the different classes of a community separately. Not long ago, I invited young men to listen to such counsels as it seemed to me they would find it useful to heed. Sunday before last, I used the freedom of this place in pointing out to the other sex, of the same age, some of their dangers and duties. This morning, I beg the privilege of speaking to such of their elders as sustain the maternal relation. Very likely you will find in my remarks little that is *new;* indeed, *can* what is new, at the same time true and pertinent, be said by any one on this subject? But I hope, nevertheless, to offer some suggestions that will be useful.

Let me begin with observing, that they who have carefully looked into the world with a view to ascertain how the human character is formed, generally agree, that the father's influence, in this respect, is neither so great nor so enduring as that of the mother. So true, indeed, does this seem to me, that I cannot but feel quite certain, that, if we knew the early history of the eminent men and women who have most adorned and benefited the world, we might follow back the stream of their usefulness and fame to the nursery, — the pure fountain of maternal prudence, affection, and piety. Nor is it strange that so it should be. Providence itself seems to have ordained, that the care of the child shall chiefly devolve on the mother. Her influence, whatever it be, whether for good or for evil, is therefore more felt than that of the father, in the most susceptible period of human existence. The infant's first smile is drawn forth by her kindness, or its first bad passion is awakened by her severity. She, too, from her greater intimacy, is better able to know the discipline it needs than the father. The earliest dawning of reason, the earliest stirring of emotion, the earliest line of character, are noticed by her quick eye. Her familiarity removes all restraint, and she can distinctly perceive the very inmost workings of the heart and mind of her offspring. From morning till evening, her eye follows the object of her hopes and fears; so that she has constant opportunities of checking every symptom of folly, encouraging every appearance of virtue, and, generally, of suiting her lessons to all the varying tempers and needs of the child. On the contrary, man, engaged in the turmoil of business, the cares of a profession, or some of the other harassing pursuits of the world, returns home, rather to relax his mind by caressing and sporting with his little ones, than to search for faults in them, or to correct their errors. His coming is generally greeted with delight in the domestic circle; and it seems to him hard to act the part of a rigid censor, to cast a gloom over cheerful faces, or chill the warm current of glad feeling in happy hearts, even in case he really discerns occasions for reproof. But in fact, nine cases out of ten, he knows less of the actual disposition of his youngest children, and of the treatment they should receive, than the chief domestic of his house; while the mother is acquainted with both the disposition and the treatment. Then, again, if we look to the commencement of learning, it is upon this same parent that the task of teaching must devolve. To say nothing of the husband's want of time; her patience, her perseverance, and her affection alone are equal to the irksome duties of that weary season, — irksome, even where nature has been most bountiful, but peculiarly trying where she has been sparing of her gifts. And then in sickness, in all the various diseases incident to childhood, who to sustain the drooping head, to administer the healing medicine, to watch the feverish slumber, to bear with all the untoward peevishness of youthful suffering, — who, but that same kind and unwearied friend, the Christian mother?

Fully, therefore, am I convinced, that in respect to the care and culture of children, upon which depends so essentially the weal or woe of subsequent years, mothers have, by far, a more difficult and important task to perform than fathers. No young person (and I would to God that I could imprint this sentiment indelibly upon every youthful mind) can ever be sufficiently grateful to a good mother, nor sufficiently thankful to a benignant Providence, if he has been blessed with such a parent. But if thus inestimable be the advantage of maternal affection regulated by prudence, and of maternal wisdom animated by piety, the evil accruing to children from a weak or wicked mother is equally incalculable. Of all the calamities which could befall an unfortunate family, that of an indiscreet, negligent, and vicious mother would seem to me the greatest.

The importance of the subject, my hearers, justifies me in addressing to such as sustain the maternal relation some very plain and earnest remarks respecting the opportunities, trusts, and duties of the responsible stations they occupy.

1. First, then, let me beg of you to consider the susceptibility of the human mind and heart in the earliest stage of life. Reflect on what edu-

cation can do for your offspring. Think not that they come from their Maker with a corrupt nature, incapable of being moulded by your hand to virtue. True, they are not perfect; true, they are inclined to evil as well as to good; and this should add to your vigilance and exertions. Regard them in a proper light. Consider that they have within them the elements of future actions, — of virtues and vices, which may raise them to honor, or sink them in disgrace. But, at the same time, view their minds and hearts as subjects of culture; as soils which may be greatly enriched, and into which you may cast good seed, with the assurance, that, with continued care on your part, and under God's common providence, it may yield the best of fruits. Remember that there is no being on earth so little what nature made it as man. It is education that chiefly forms his principles and habits; and these almost invariably remain with him through life: so that he is, in the end, much more that which he has become than that which he was created. What a lesson is this fact suited to teach mothers, and, indeed, all who have in any way the oversight and guidance of the young! True, a single folly encouraged, a single evil passion suffered to triumph, a single vicious habit permitted to strengthen itself, may one day terminate in melancholy results; but it is more than equally true, that from pure sentiments and noble conduct, early secured by right culture, we may confidently expect the happiest consequences in mature life and old age.

2. In the next place, reflect, I beseech you, on the greatness of the trust reposed in such as sustain a relation like yours to children and youth. Be it that you do not sit in the councils of the nation; but you have the first agency in forming the legislators who are to guide the destinies of our country. Be it that you do not occupy the judge's bench, nor enter the jury box; yet both the balance and the sword of justice are indirectly controlled by you, through early maternal teaching. Be it that you do not engage in commerce; but you mould the characters of those upon whose talents and upright dealing the prosperity, reputation, and happiness, both of individuals and the community, very much depends. What responsibleness, therefore, rests upon you! The welfare of thousands may be traced to the good disposition and virtuous character of a single mother; for her influence often reaches to many generations. If she is as she should be, she may be the means of diffusing over a wide circle, born and unborn, the inestimable blessings of religion and morality, of honest and successful industry, of usefulness to society, and joyous peace in private life. My friends, think of this, and redouble your exertions to fulfil well the responsible stations you occupy. Let

no concern seem to you so great and urgent as that of rightly training the children whom Providence hath committed, during their forming period, to your charge. Better fail in any or all things else than in the work of early education, — better for yourselves, and better for your sons and daughters!

3. Again, let me request you to consider, that a mother's respectability and true honor lie in her personal attention to the welfare of her offspring. She who imagines that any cause, save that of inability, may exempt her from the duties of parental vigilance and instruction, strangely miscalculates the nature of her office; and she who looks upon it as a degradation to become the instructor of her own offspring is a stranger to that which would constitute the highest dignity of her sex. In the walks of fashion she may shine; her qualities may excite the envy of some, and command the respect of others; her accomplishments may secure the admiration of many, and swell her own heart with vanity: but, after all, such is not the true scene of either her interest, respectability, or happiness. The sphere of her substantial, unfading honor lies far away from the crowded haunts of frivolous amusement, even in the peaceful retreat of her home. There, in the midst of her children, she represses the frowardness of one, encourages the diffidence of another, and, in judiciously familiar phrase and

wisely adapted story, pours lessons of instruction into the minds of all. With a mother's gentleness, she draws forth their talents; with a mother's firmness, she regulates their tempers; with a mother's prudence, she prepares them to adorn their stations upon earth; and, with a mother's piety, she leads them in the path towards heaven. The wide world presents no object more interesting, more exalted, or more useful, than such a Christian parent; nor is there any spot on which the eye of God rests with greater complacency than upon the retired and peaceful scene of her virtuous labors. Such a mother becomes the centre of a system of honorable usefulness, of whose extent the imagination can form no adequate conception; for there is not a single worthy principle which she instils, that may not descend as the ornament and solace of many generations.

I have spoken of the susceptibility of childhood to a mother's influence; I have spoken of the responsibleness of a mother's station; I have spoken of the respectability of a mother's legitimate duties.

These duties it is not my aim — indeed, it is not within the compass of my ability — to state and explain in detail. They are as numerous as your thoughts, feelings, and actions; for all these, in one way or another, have a direct or an indirect bearing on your children's character, and, through them, on the community. But I can, and with your leave I will briefly, suggest how, or in what spirit, these duties should be performed.

1. First, then, seek to perform them intelligently. For this end, give your minds to study, — to the study, I especially mean, of human nature, and of the art of education. Think not that you gained wisdom enough of this sort at school. No knowledge, as to these points, can be too extensive for the right management of children. Even in the most subordinate mechanical employment, the artisan requires to understand the proper use of his implements, and the nature of the materials upon which he is to operate. And, surely, a Christian mother, whose mind is a waste or a wilderness, must be unfitted for enlarging the understandings, cultivating the dispositions, regulating the principles, and forming the habits of her offspring. In truth, such a mother is doubly unqualified for her station: first, by incapacity; and, next, in being unable to secure that filial respect which is essential to the due efficacy of all parental instruction.

2. Secondly, discharge the duties of your office affectionately. All mean to do this, I doubt not. Yet many, through inadvertence or a bad temper, fail of it. Parents are often not aware how soon children discern and begin to partake of the spirit that rules in the breast of those who have the care of them. You may see it frequently almost

in their first smile or in their first tear. It is quite surprising how early the infant can read the disposition of the heart in the expression of the countenance. Long before it can either speak or understand a single word of language, the little observer can detect the sentiments of the soul in the features of the face or in the tones of the voice. And no sooner does it discover than it begins to copy them. How important, therefore, that a mother's temper, and her manifestations of it, be habitually what they should be, — mild, cheerful, bland, and affectionate! Even with regard to a froward child, such feeling and demeanor in a parent, when connected, as they ought always to be, with firmness of purpose, are the most effectual remedy of juvenile depravities. They are as coals of a purifying fire, which, laid upon valuable ore, melt and send out the precious metal in glowing and copious streams, while the dross, gradually consumed, at last wholly disappears.

3. Finally, let me say, — and with emphasis, — perform the maternal duties of education religiously. "As is the mother, so is the daughter," saith the Bible: and so also, let me add, is the son, to a very great extent; and this respecting the most important of all points, namely, piety and virtue. When I see a highly moral and religious young man or woman, it occurs to me, as a natural and obvious reflection, that the mother's

character was distinguished very much in the same way. I use the word *character*, because it implies and includes, not only what is outward in conduct, but the heart's genuine sentiments and the life's actual conduct; and these are needful to constitute an example, in a parent, that will work favorably upon the children. *Example*,— this it is which does the work; but then it must be the example of *thought* as well as of word, of *feeling* as well as of profession. Little good shall we do our little boys and girls, merely by teaching them how to say, "Our Father who art in heaven," if, in fact, we pray not ourselves; nor can we benefit them much by talking of the worth of the Bible and of the Sabbath, while we ourselves neglect both the one and the other. Children know the difference between reality and sham. When, therefore, I said, perform the maternal duties *religiously*, I of course meant something more than following a form of piety, be it of this church or of that. Nothing less than this did I intend; namely, that the mother should, from the first, cherish in her own heart, and exhibit in all, even her minutest, actions, before her sons and daughters, a profound reverence for God, a deep sentiment of love for his Son Jesus Christ, and a sincerely respectful regard for religious institutions. Great wisdom, however, is here needed. Let the mother be careful, neither inwardly to feel, nor outwardly to show, that religion is a separate, exclusive, unsocial, gloomy thing. Her religion she must have as a spring of gladness in her own soul; and she must carry it about with her, always and everywhere, as a help to the making of others joyful. In commending it to her children, she should aim to connect it with all that is most interesting to their hearts; so that it may be, even without their knowing it, early incorporated with their most delightful sentiments, and interwoven with their dearest associations.

But I must stop here. A great deal might be added: time, however, would fail me, should I attempt to say more. The discourse has been addressed to a most influential class of the community, and, I hope, not wholly in vain. There is no relation in life more important than the maternal. God grant that all who sustain it amongst us may feel their responsibility, and perform their duties intelligently, affectionately, and religiously! "What is most wanted," asked Napoleon, one day, of a distinguished female friend, — "what is most wanted, in order that the youth of France may be well educated?" — "Good mothers," was her reply. There could not have been more wisdom condensed into so few words. The aggregate influence of mothers is greater than all the rest which operate to form the character of a people. The fathers of New England are often eulogized; but, in truth, the virtue and piety of our communities is owing more to the early mothers than the early fathers. Honored be their memories! Shall New England *continue* to take the lead in morals and religion, as well as in intelligence? This can and will be only on the condition, that in the future, as in the past, she is blessed with "good mothers."

IX.

MAN AND TRUE MANLINESS.

Psalm viii. 3, 4, 5: "WHEN I CONSIDER THE HEAVENS, THE WORK OF THY FINGERS, THE MOON AND THE STARS WHICH THOU HAST ORDAINED, — WHAT IS MAN THAT THOU ART MINDFUL OF HIM? AND THE SON OF MAN, THAT THOU VISITEST HIM? FOR THOU HAST MADE HIM A LITTLE LOWER THAN THE ANGELS, AND HAST CROWNED HIM WITH GLORY AND HONOR."

THE first natural sentiment which awakens within us, as we contemplate the vastness of the universe, and God's infinite power and greatness, is the one expressed in the beginning of the text, — a feeling that creatures so small as we can hardly be among the objects of divine regard; and we are moved to exclaim, "What is man, O God! that thou art mindful of him?" But as with David, so with us: this sentiment is soon succeeded by another more elevating and ennobling. Our thoughts, though they must recognize, cannot dwell on, man's comparative insignificance. They rise above it. They hasten to the consideration of his intrinsic nature, his own high capacities and powers, his real importance, his positive relations to God and immortality; and we are then prompted to adopt again the appropriate language of the Psalmist,—"Thou hast made us a little lower than the angels, and hast crowned us with glory and honor." And so to do is not only natural and right: it is also useful.

My hearers, among man's many wants is the want of a true self-respect. He has been told so much of his weakness and depravity, that he has almost come to believe there is little else save weakness and depravity in his nature. Would it not be good for him to be reminded more frequently of his higher endowments? At least, ought not the distinction to be kept carefully in view, between what he is as he comes from his Creator's hand, and what he makes himself by his vices?

There are two ways of treating children at school: one is to be always telling them that they are dunces, and cannot learn; the other is to impress it on their minds, at proper seasons, that they have capacities and powers for valuable acquisitions. The latter method, it seems to me, is the better one. So, as regards mankind at large, there are two modes of addressing them on moral and religious subjects: the one is to talk to them perpetually of a supposed entire corruption of the human heart by nature, and thus to depress and discourage them; the other is to remind them often of the capabilities God hath given them for high attainments in piety and virtue. Do I err in deeming the latter mode preferable to the former?

Far be it from me, however, to think or speak EXTRAVAGANTLY of human nature: but, surely, what Scripture and reason authorize I may believe respecting it; and teach too, if by so doing any good practical end can be accomplished.

Men want, as I have said, a true self-respect. Perhaps there is nothing, except reverence for God, that some persons more need than this. But no one can have it who sees in his nature only weakness, impurity, and vice. And destitute of all due self-respect, having never learned to appreciate aright his natural capabilities, a man lacks one of the most effectual of moving forces. Inaction accompanies imagined impotency. Effort, if ever made, follows the belief that effort will avail something. What can reasonably be expected of one who deems himself akin to the brute? or of him who believes he was created with an irresistible proneness to sin, and with capacities and tastes for nothing else? If I wished to reduce a community to the lowest condition of vice, I should begin with trying to make its members think meanly of their nature; with attempting to convince them that man is little more than a common animal, except that he has somewhat greater ingenuity and power for mischief. Among the steps of discipline by which an individual ascends in improvement towards perfection, one of the most important, in my opinion, is, that he learn early in life to respect himself, to think worthily of what, as a human being, he was created to be, and may become; and the teacher can hardly do a better service, than to heighten in the community this sense of character, this feeling of a superior nature, this consciousness of moral capacity and power.

Nor let it be feared that hereby the grounds of Christian humility will be removed. To respect one's self, in the sense intended, is not the same as being satisfied with one's acquired character; but it is simply to think justly, i.e. highly, of one's original nature. To form too lofty conceptions of what we have made ourselves is one thing, and certainly a bad thing. But it is quite another, and altogether a good thing, to respect, to deem sacred, to reverence most profoundly, what God hath made us. Christian humility grows out of the conviction of having *neglected or abused* divine gifts, not of having never received them. It follows, that the true way to make a man feel humble is, not to teach him that the nature he has in common with his race is a mean one; but it is to show him, that, whatever be this nature of his, he has acted unworthily of it. Persuade a person who is conscious of great moral deficiencies that his original capabilities were of a high order, and you adopt the most effectual means of giving him the true feeling of humility; because you lead him to reflect on what he was created to be and might have become, in contrast with what he knows that he is. Indeed, the more a man reverences his nature, other things being alike, so much the more humbling must be his sense of personal failings and imperfections: and, let me add, the more highly one thinks of his nature, provided he keeps within the bounds of truth, so much the more likely will he be, other things being equal, to improve; for such a man, as a matter of course, elevates the mark at which he aims, from what has been done to what may be done; and, if he do not reach perfection, he is sure to approach nearer to it for constantly keeping it in his view.

But the subject of the text, — "MAN"? How much, brethren, is implied in this little word of but three letters! Who comprehends its entire meaning? Be it, as many love to suggest, that this creature, called *man*, is often to be seen in conditions not very well suited to inspire reverence, — in the cradle, in the forest, in the prison. But what follows? That his *nature* is at fault? Why point me to the infant, the savage, the criminal? They afford no fair specimen of man's true capacities and powers. I see in them immaturity, or want of cultivation, or unfaithfulness; but no lack of natural ability for that which is good and great. What was man *designed* to be, what *can* he be, what *is* he, when, under appropriate circumstances, all his native powers are entirely and proportionably unfolded? Answer these questions aright, and you give me correct views of human nature. In a word, the nature of man is to be learned, not from studying it in its uncultivated or abused state, but in its condition of full growth and perfection. Now, take such a specimen; take a man whose whole physical, intellectual, moral, and religious character is, as it was intended to be, full-grown, completely developed, perfected; and what, I ask, amongst the works of God, is so worthy of admiration? Who does not feel compelled, with the Psalmist, to exclaim, "Thou hast made him a little lower than the angels, and crowned him with glory and honor"? What power of thought! What strength of affection! What noble deeds! Reason, conscious free will, — what wonders these! He conceives of God! He feels himself immortal! And this is the nature, which it is our charge, not to despise, but to reverence; not to degrade, but to exalt; not to stint and sully, but to enrich and adorn. Brethren, do we accept the charge? and are we willing to obey it? Then, happily, we are in a mood to form and express, as becomes us, conceptions and purposes of duty, befitting the devout and grateful acknowledgment of the text, "Thou hast made us a little lower than the angels, and hast crowned us with glory and honor."

"Thou hast made us a little lower than the angels." Then, God helping us, we will rise at once above the sphere of animals. Such beings as we should scorn to seek their chief good in sensual indulgence. Appetite and passion, then, let us control; and, looking beyond this body, recognize the mind; and pass life, not in asking, chiefly, what shall we eat, what shall we drink, wherewithal shall we be clothed, but in cultivating to the utmost that in us which is distinctively human.

"Thou hast made us a little lower than the angels." Then shame on us, if we allow ourselves to be passively shaped by outward circumstances, or to be the creatures of accidental impulse, or to be carried hither and thither by the ever-varying currents of the times! For, clearly enough, it belongs to our nature to have a will — subordinate to God's indeed, yet our own, and as responsible as it is personal — to act this way or that, not because others do so, nor from motives of worldly policy, but conscientiously, from a principle, a spring, an energy within, which is an overmatch for adverse influences from without; which makes external things yield before us; which enables us to resist the force of circumstances, and to bend events to our own high purposes.

"Thou hast made us a little lower than the angels." Then let us see to it, that our individuality and independence be not lost amidst earth-serving multitudes that may chance to gather around us. For God created every man, even as he did the angel, not to disappear in the crowd, not merely to make part of a whole, not to help compose a mass as a particle of dust in a sand-hill; but he created each of us a distinct, ultimate being, and constituted his own perfection his highest end, and ordained accordingly that he should have his appropriate share, stand upon his own feet, maintain a separate existence, act a peculiar part, and form a distinctive character.

"Thou hast made us a little lower than the angels." Then no timidity, no fear, becomes us, except that of doing wrong. Ours must be a spirit that nothing in this world's artificial glare and glory can awe or abash; a spirit that feels itself accountable to a higher tribunal than the popular judgment; that respects itself too much to be the slave of any fashion, or the tool of any party; that is frightened from the narrow way of right by no difficulty, reproach, or peril, but adheres to duty, bold in the presence of danger, calm in the midst of tumult, self-possessed and determined, though all seem adverse, save conscience and God.

"Thou hast made us a little lower than the

angels." How, then, can we think of living to ourselves alone? Shall we disgrace our own high nature by caring nothing for the same nature in our fellows? God forbid, that so we should shut up and quench in selfish souls that divine principle of love within us, which, quickened and expanded as it was designed to be, knows no bounds to its benevolence; which recognizes in all human beings the image of God and the rights of his children; which rejoices in virtue wherever found, and sympathizes with suffering wherever seen; which vanquishes pride and selfishness and indolence, and offers itself up, if need be, a willing sacrifice on the broad altar of society!

"Thou hast made us a little lower than the angels." Then far from our mind, let us at once say, be every inordinate desire of those worldly distinctions, which, either in the attaining or in the possessing of them, will put to hazard our integrity, our peace of mind, our usefulness, or our spiritual advancement! For what to us should be wealth, if, in the getting of it, we must lose our health or our virtue, or in the using of it must grow voluptuous? What to us should be office, if the way to it lead us through corruption, and the station itself is surrounded with all that perplexes and debases? What to us should be leisure, that boon so much coveted, if, in having it, we must think of no concern on earth but to live easily, having nothing to do but pamper and adorn the body, or chase frivolous pleasures, or flutter gayly about society, — the most insignificant and useless thing in God's world? And so of the rest, — as we have within us each a living human soul, — away with them all, so far, I mean, as they interfere with the functions and growth of that soul! For why despoil our better nature of its Creator's image while living, and, in dying, leave behind us no memorial of our privileged existence, except, perhaps, some few stones over our grave, and some few words of an epitaph, which, if true, can but remind passers-by that we were rich, or were once in office, or were gentlemen of leisure, and did nobody any good, but much harm to many, at least through our example, — when we might live a life, might perform deeds, might build up characters, the memory of which would be enshrined in the hearts of thousands on earth for their spiritual good, while ourselves were enjoying the bliss of heaven?

"Thou hast made us a little lower than the angels." Then, my hearers, I end, as I began, by saying, we need self-respect; and, in order to have it, we must know and feel something of the greatness which pertains to the nature God hath given to us. From this doctrine many doubtless will dissent; and some believers in it, very likely, may question the expediency of making it a frequent topic of instruction. For myself, I belong no more to the latter class than to the former. The doctrine seems to me not only true, but of great practical use; and the prevalent modes of thought and action show that there is urgent need of its being often inculcated. Who can believe that the mass of mankind would conduct themselves so unworthily as they do, but for the low notions they have been taught to entertain of the nature whereof they are partakers? How can they be elevated in morals and religion, except it be impressed upon their minds that they have capacities and powers for high attainments,—that *it is in them* to rise to eminence in piety and virtue? As for thee, my brother, my sister, whoever thou mayst be that hearest me, if thou feelest within thy soul any sincere desire to be and do all that, and only that, which becomes thee, then, first of all, know and understand what God hath created thee, what he hath taught thee to aspire after, and what thou canst, under him, make thyself. It will be one of thy best safeguards against vice, and one of the most efficient quickeners of virtue. Learn, betimes, to think well of thy nature; not, however, as if this could imply unconsciousness of transgression. No: abhor thy sins, cast them far from thee, lament in dust and ashes thy shortcomings, and bow in all contrition and humility before the throne of divine grace; but never,

never blame human nature, whatever may be thy own character; remember Him who made it what it is, and honor the Creator by respecting his work. Next to God and his Son Jesus Christ, reverence thy nature; stand in awe of it; rejoice and be grateful in thinking of its noble powers, its lofty aspirations. Guard it from error and pollution more than thou wouldst the safety of a thousand lives, hadst thou so many to protect. Turn away from those who would rob thee of the conviction, that thou hast within thee, as the gift of an all-wise and benevolent God, capacities and principles which ally thee to the spirits on high. Crave association with those who recognize and delight to speak of the native greatness, the immortal growth, of the human soul. At all times, and in all places, remember, or, if thou chance to forget it, seek to be reminded as soon as possible, that a mere animal thou art not, but a being of a high order, made a little lower than the angels, created in the image of God and his own eternity; and, with full comprehension of what this language of Holy Writ means, see to it that thou act up to all which it implies.

X.

Job v. 26: "THOU SHALT COME TO THY GRAVE IN A FULL AGE, LIKE AS A SHOCK OF CORN COMETH IN ITS SEASON."

[The following is an extract from a discourse occasioned by the death of John Wheeler, Esq., for many years a much-respected parishioner of Dr. Barrett's, who died in 1856, aged 76. After discoursing on some of the consolations under bereavement from the death of aged friends, the sermon closed with the following suggestions as to the means by which a good old age could be secured.]

LIVE temperately. Eat not too much. Drink not too much. Indulge not the passions too much. By neglect in these respects, multitudes lay the foundation of disease, and bring on a premature death.

Live calmly. Let nothing greatly disturb you. Next to temperance, as to the bodily appetite, equanimity is one of the chief helpers to a long life. Fret not. Guard against being chafed by the world. Transact your business quietly. Avoid extremes in every pursuit. Follow the golden mean, always and everywhere. Neither rust out in indolence, nor wear out by too much work. Be not over-anxious about health, or any thing else. Nothing wastes one's strength more surely than the thousand vexations to which many allow themselves to be subject; while nothing leads more certainly to a full age than tranquil equanimity in good and in bad fortune.

Live constantly on your guard against needless exposures. Presume not that you are able to bear up under every possible burden of business. Know and feel that the most robust body cannot endure all things; that extremes of heat and cold are not to be encountered without appropriate safeguards; that excessive toil will in time break down the firmest frame; that slight sicknesses, brought on by whatever cause, are not to be disregarded, but attended to in season; that health, in a word, is as fragile as it is precious, and, for its continuance to a full age, must be thoughtfully cared for and protected from a thousand foes by its possessors.

Live in all respects virtuously and piously. So to do is to obey the laws of nature and of God; and to obey this law is the true method of attaining to a full age. Virtue and piety comprise the sum of human duty; and in the way of duty is safety, — safety to the physical as well as the spiritual part of man. Duty, done seasonably and faithfully, all of duty, — what is it, but the fit regulation of the thoughts, the right government of the feelings, the keeping of one's self unspotted from the world, the avoidance of all vice, the practice of morality in its every department, the love and worship of God, the following of Christ in purity and all excellence, the cherishing of good-will towards every human being, the possessing and exercising of a conscience void of offence at all times and in all places, the maintaining and manifesting of a cheerful and hopeful spirit in respect both to this world and the next? And who will say that these things, and such as these, are not favorable to health and longevity?

But I need not proceed further. Believing as I do that the fulness of age is a privilege and blessing to the good, I wish and pray for it, as it concerns both you and myself, in the hope that we shall do what is necessary on our part to secure it.

Especially do I wish and pray for a *happy* fulness of age, as was that of him who has lately departed from amongst us. God, in his infinite mercy, fulfil the wish! May the close of your life, brothers and sisters, be calm and peaceful! May memory then place before you a pleasing picture of the past! May faith stand before you, like an angel of light, to make the future as a blissful reality! May friendship hang over you with all the benignity and tenderness of a ministering spirit! while gratitude, at a distance, points to her heart, and tells you, "There shall you be interred." Yes, my friends, this I sincerely wish for you, and all besides which will supply a mild and cheerful light to the evening of your day, when its gaudier beams shall be gone; all which will irradiate the shadows of your dying hours.

Especially the remembrance of such a uniform and constant career of virtuous conduct as shall, in conjunction with the mercy of God, in Jesus Christ, lay a foundation for the steady and unhesitating hope of rising from the body that dies to the life everlasting in heaven.

THE END.

Cambridge: Printed by John Wilson & Son.

List of Publications

ISSUED AND FOR SALE BY

WILLIAM V. SPENCER,

203 Washington Street, Boston.

☞ *The usual Discount to the Trade.* ☜

ANDERSON (I. H.) Patriotism at Home; or, The Young Invincibles. By the author of "Fred Freeland." With Four Illustrations, from original designs by CHAMPNEY. Printed on heavy paper, in handsome binding. 1 vol. 16mo. Price $1.50.

BERRY (MRS. M. E.) Celesta. A Girl's Book. 16mo. In press. $1.25.

——— Crooked and Straight. 16mo. In press. $1.25.

BRADLEE (MISS). Christus Victor. A Poem. Square 16mo. Flexible cloth. 50 cts.

——— Max Overman. 16mo. Paper. 50 cts.

——— Three Crowns. 16mo. Cloth. $1.25.

BULFINCH (REV. S. G., D. D.) Manual of the Evidences of Christianity. For Classes and Private Reading. 12mo. $1.25.

CALVERT (G. H.) Some of the Thoughts of JOSEPH JOUBERT. With a Biographical Notice. 16mo. Tinted paper. Cloth, bevelled. $1.50.

——— First Years in Europe. By the author of "Scenes and Thoughts in Europe," "The Gentleman," &c. 1 vol. 12mo. $1.75.

A finished and attractive narrative of a residence in Antwerp, Gottingen, Weimar, Edinburgh, and Paris, forty years ago; abounding in powerful criticisms of the religious and political sentiment of that time, exhibiting a close study of the literature and a familiar acquaintance with the literary men of that age.

CARPENTER (MISS MARY). Our Convicts. 2 vols. in 1. pp. 293 and 380. Octavo. $4.50.

CHANNING (MISS E. P.) The Adventures of a German Toy. A charming story for children, with three Illustrations. 75 cts.

COBBE (Frances Power). Religious Duty. 12mo. Cloth, bevelled sides. $1.75.

——— Studies New and Old, of Ethical and Social Subjects. Crown 8vo. Price $3.00.

Contents: Christian Ethics and the Ethics of Christ; Self-Development and Self-Abnegation; The Sacred Books of the Zoroastrians; The Philosophy of the Poor Laws; The Rights of Man and the Claims of Brutes; The Morals of Literature; The Hierarchy of Art; Decemnovenarianism; Hades.

FERNALD (Rev. W. M.) God in his Providence. 12mo. Cloth. $1.50.

——— A View at the Foundations; or, First Causes of Character. 12mo. Cloth. $1.00.

GREY (Hester). Kitty Barton. A simple Story for Children. With One Illustration. 32mo. 60 cts.

HOLLISTER (G. H.) Thomas à Becket. A Tragedy, and other Poems. 16mo. $1.75.

LINCOLNIANA. In one vol., small quarto. pp. viii. and 344. $6.00. (Only 250 copies printed.)

MARTINEAU (Jas.) Essays: Philosophical and Theological. Crown Octavo. Tinted paper. $2.50.

☞ Other volumes of the series in preparation.

MILL (John Stuart). Dissertations and Discussions. 3 vols. 12mo. Cloth. Per vol., $2.25.

——— The Examination of the Philosophy of Sir William Hamilton. 2 vols. 12mo. Cloth. Per vol., $2.25.

——— The Positive Philosophy of Auguste Comte. 1 vol. 12mo. Cloth. $1.25.

MUZZEY (Rev. A. B.) The Blade and the Ear. Thoughts for a Young Man. 16mo. Red edges, bevelled sides, $1.50; plain, $1.25.

NAVILLE (Ernest). The Heavenly Father: Lectures on Modern Atheism. By Ernest Naville, late Professor of Philosophy in the University of Geneva. Translated from the French, by Henry Dornton, M. A. Published in a handsome 16mo volume. $1.75.

"A thorough grappling with some of the most subtle and profound questions of the age. 'The Revival of Atheism,' &c. The author is thoroughly evangelical, and has treated his subjects with a masterly scholarship and ability. We hail all such books as the fulfilment of the Scripture promise, 'When the enemy shall come in like a flood, the spirit of the Lord shall lift up a standard against him.'"

REED (Wm. Howell). Hospital Life in the Army of the Potomac. 16mo. $1.25.

STAHR (Adolf). The Life and Works of Gotthold Ephraim Lessing. Translated from the German of Adolf Stahr, by E. P. Evans, Ph. D., Michigan University. 2 vols. Crown octavo. $5.00.

THURSTON (Mrs. Elizabeth A.) The Little Wrinkled Old Man. A Christmas Extravaganza, and other Trifles. Illustrated. 75 cts.

TOWLE (Geo. M.) Glimpses of History. 1 vol. 16mo. Bevelled boards. $1.50.

TOWNSEND (Miss Virginia F.) Darryll Gap; or, Whether it Paid. A Novel. 1 vol. 12mo. pp. 456. $1.75.

A book of great force and power, dealing with the follies, the errors, and the extravagance of this great sensational age. Depicting life among those who have suddenly acquired wealth, and displaying lessons of devotion and self-sacrifice, drawn from a new field, hitherto untrod by the novelist. The *Boston Transcript* says of it: —

"The story is thoroughly American in tone, scenery, incident, and characters; it is to American life what Miss Bremer's 'Home' is to life in Sweden. Like the Swedish tale, simple, natural in incident, its characters have each a powerful individuality which takes hold at once upon the interest and sympathies of the reader. The drama of the story is artistic, and though its materials are drawn from the simple, human, every-day life of our homes, the power of the book is felt to its close; the moral lessons it unobtrusively teaches, cannot fail to sink deep into the hearts of all who read it."

WARE (Rev. J. F. W.) Home Life: What it Is, and What it Needs. 16mo. Cloth. Red edges, bevelled sides. $1.25.

Recently Issued.

REASON IN RELIGION: By F. H. Hedge, D.D. 1 vol. Crown octavo. $2.00.

NEW WORKS JUST ISSUED.

LOVE IN SPAIN, AND OTHER POEMS. By Martha Perry Lowe. 1 vol. 16mo. $1.50.

SERMONS: By Rev. E. B. Hall, D.D., Pastor of the First Congregational Church, Providence, R.I., from 1832 to 1867. With a brief Memoir. 1 vol. 16mo. $1.25.

FIRST HISTORICAL TRANSFORMATIONS OF CHRISTIANITY. From the French of Athanase Coquerel the Younger. By E. P. Evans, Ph.D., Michigan University. 1 vol. 16mo. $1.50.

*** Copies sent by mail, free of postage, on receipt of price.

THE LIFE AND WORKS

OF

LESSING.

TRANSLATED FROM THE GERMAN OF ADOLPH STAHR, BY E. P. EVANS, PH. D., MICHIGAN UNIVERSITY.

Two volumes. Crown octavo. Price $5.00.

"A work of permanent value. . . . It is the best of many books which have been written and compiled for the purpose of portraying the character and career of one of the most illustrious scholars and thinkers that even Germany has produced. It combines judicious selection with ample information, criticism with narration, and presents with comparative brevity an outline of labors, the benefits of which the world is now enjoying in almost every department of learning and culture. . . . The translation is excellent."—*Nation, New York.*

"The position of Lessing in German literature renders him the subject of peculiar interest among those who have at heart a sound intellectual culture in this country. We are thankful to Professor Evans for presenting to our countrymen the biography of such a man in so handsome a form. . . . We can safely predict to our readers that the perusal of the volumes will give them a fresh sympathy with a man whose name has to a great extent been the subject of vague association rather than positive knowledge, and will throw new light on the fortunes of the great battle for freedom and truth in the last century."—*New York Tribune.*

"As a literary biography, it is one of the best specimens which has appeared in many years, and seems to have been a labor of love to both author and translator. We commend these handsome, valuable, and interesting volumes to all inquiring, progressive, and sympathetic minds, and all readers who would become familiar with the noblest type of literary life."—*N Y. Independent.*

"Stahr's biography of Lessing, which he has so admirably translated in these volumes, was the result of 'twenty years of earnest and enthusiastic study.' It is an elaborate account of Lessing's life, works and times, influence and contemporaries, and is a valuable contribution to the literary history of Germany."—*Boston Transcript.*

"A highly honorable contribution to American letters."—*N. Y. Tribune.*

For sale by all booksellers. Copies sent by mail free of postage, on receipt of retail price.

A liberal discount allowed to libraries, students, and clergymen.

WILLIAM V. SPENCER,

PUBLISHER,

203 Washington Street, corner of Bromfield.

www.ingramcontent.com/pod-product-compliance
Lightning Source LLC
LaVergne TN
LVHW011204110826
845150LV00006B/1312

* 9 7 8 1 4 2 5 5 1 8 7 6 9 *